PRAISE FOR MIKE SCHMOKER'S PREVIOUS

P9-CQJ-620

FOCUS

Few writers on education ever get close to the clarity provided by Mike Schmoker. . . . Read it and be amazed.
–Jay Mathews, education columnist for the *Washington Post* and author of *Work Hard. Be Nice: How Two Inspired Teachers Created the Most Promising Schools in America*

Not only easily understood but translates into immediate action.
–Robert J. Marzano, C.E.O. of Marzano Research Laboratory and author of *The Art and Science of Teaching: A Comprehensive Framework for Effective Instruction*

Mike Schmoker nails it again.
–Carol Jago, president of the National Council of Teachers of English

A book to which many teachers will say "Hallelujah." . . . If we can get our schools focused on the elements Schmoker identifies, more teachers will be achieving dramatic results in their classrooms.
–David T. Conley, director of the Center for Educational Policy Research, University of Oregon

Mike Schmoker says all we need to know.
–Grant Wiggins, president of Authentic Education and coauthor of *Understanding by Design*

Cuts through the noise. . . . A must read for all teachers, administrators, board members, and policymakers.
–Kelly Gallagher, educator and author of *Readicide: How Schools Are Killing Reading and What You Can Do About It*

Mike Schmoker gets it right. . . . A model of how to cut through the curricular clutter.
–Gerald Graff, 2008 president of the Modern Language Association and author of *Clueless in Academe: How Schooling Obscures the Life of the Mind*

One of those books every educator needs to read.
–Dick Allington, educator and author of *What Really Matters for Struggling Readers: Designing Research-Based Programs*

LEADING WITH
FOCUS

ASCD MEMBER BOOK

Many ASCD members received this book as a
member benefit upon its initial release.

Learn more at: **www.ascd.org/memberbooks**

LEADING WITH
FOCUS

Elevating the Essentials
for School and District
Improvement

MIKE SCHMOKER

ASCD | Alexandria, VA USA

1703 N. Beauregard St. • Alexandria, VA 22311-1714 USA
Phone: 800-933-2723 or 703-578-9600 • Fax: 703-575-5400
Website: www.ascd.org • E-mail: member@ascd.org
Author guidelines: www.ascd.org/write

Deborah S. Delisle, *Executive Director,* Stefani Roth, *Publisher;* Genny Ostertag, *Director, Content Acquisitions;* Julie Houtz, *Director, Book Editing & Production;* Ernesto Yermoli, *Editor;* Lindsey Smith, *Senior Graphic Designer;* Mike Kalyan, *Manager, Production Services;* Keith Demmons, *Production Designer;* Kelly Marshall, *Production Specialist*

Copyright © 2016 ASCD. All rights reserved. It is illegal to reproduce copies of this work in print or electronic format (including reproductions displayed on a secure intranet or stored in a retrieval system or other electronic storage device from which copies can be made or displayed) without the prior written permission of the publisher. By purchasing only authorized electronic or print editions and not participating in or encouraging piracy of copyrighted materials, you support the rights of authors and publishers. Readers who wish to reproduce or republish excerpts of this work in print or electronic format may do so for a small fee by contacting the Copyright Clearance Center (CCC), 222 Rosewood Dr., Danvers, MA 01923, USA (phone: 978-750-8400; fax: 978-646-8600; web: www.copyright.com). To inquire about site licensing options or any other reuse, contact ASCD Permissions at www.ascd.org/permissions, or permissions@ascd.org, or 703-575-5749. For a list of vendors authorized to license ASCD e-books to institutions, see www.ascd.org/epubs. Send translation inquiries to translations@ascd.org.

All referenced trademarks are the property of their respective owners.

All web links in this book are correct as of the publication date below but may have become inactive or otherwise modified since that time. If you notice a deactivated or changed link, please e-mail books@ascd.org with the words "Link Update" in the subject line. In your message, please specify the web link, the book title, and the page number on which the link appears.

PAPERBACK ISBN: 978-1-4166-2136-2   ASCD product #116024

PDF E-BOOK ISBN: 978-1-4166-2138-6; see Books in Print for other formats.

Quantity discounts: 10–49, 10%; 50+, 15%; 1,000+, special discounts (e-mail programteam@ascd.org or call 800-933-2723, ext. 5773, or 703-575-5773). For desk copies, go to www.ascd.org/deskcopy.

ASCD Member Book No. FY16-4B (Jan. 2016 PSI+). ASCD Member Books mail to Premium (P), Select (S), and Institutional Plus (I+) members on this schedule: Jan, PSI+; Feb, P; Apr, PSI+; May, P; Jul, PSI+; Aug, P; Sep, PSI+; Nov, PSI+; Dec, P. For current details on membership, see www.ascd.org/membership.

Library of Congress Cataloging-in-Publication Data

Names: Schmoker, Michael J., author.
Title: Leading with focus : elevating the essentials for school and district improvement / Mike Schmoker.
Description: Alexandria, Virginia : ASCD, [2016] | Includes bibliographical references and index.
Identifiers: LCCN 2015037211 | ISBN 9781416621362 (pbk.)
Subjects: LCSH: School management and organization. | School improvement programs. | School districts--Administration.
Classification: LCC LB2805 .L38155 2016 | DDC 371.2--dc23 LC record available at http://lccn.loc.gov/2015037211

25 24 23 22 21 20 19 18 17 16   1 2 3 4 5 6 7 8 9 10 11 12

For my two daughters, Michelle and Megan, their husbands, Alex and Josh—and for their future grandchildren, whose education will depend so much on what school leaders decide to focus on in the coming decades.

*How do teaching and learning
improve? The answer is no mystery.*

—Carl Glickman

LEADING WITH
FOCUS

**Elevating the Essentials
for School and District
Improvement**

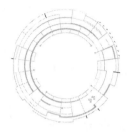

Acknowledgments

This book could not have been written without the help of the successful leaders whose work is at the core of what I advocate in this book. For years, I have wanted to capture the simple essence of what I learned from these leaders through observations and interviews. Their accomplishments and example convinced me that to be effective, school leadership needed to be drastically simplified—and its focus intensified.

I am especially grateful to the following school and district leaders (in alphabetical order): Richard DuFour, Robert Hendricks, Tim Kanold, Kim Marshall, and Susan Szachowicz. They have all been exceptionally helpful and inspiring.

I am also deeply grateful to the editors and publications team at ASCD: Stefani Roth, Carol Collins, and Ernesto Yermoli. Carol was extremely generous with her time and instrumental in nudging me to develop and refine this book. Ernesto guided the work, with grace and care, through the editing process; because of him, the book is both stronger and clearer. I am, as always, deeply appreciative of the cover art for my book, so capably provided here by Lindsey Smith.

If anything I have ever written is at all useful or clear, much of the credit goes to the influence of two of my favorite professors: Dr. James Bartell and the late Dr. Richard Wood, whose words and thoughts and time contributed so much to my development as a writer.

I am, as always, deeply grateful to my wife, Cheryl, and to my daughters, Michelle and Megan, whose love and support for me and for my work have never flagged.

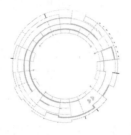

Introduction

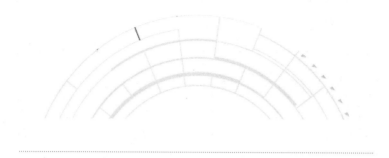

....

The first law of simplicity: Reduce.

—John Maeda

....

A rich, rounded education has profound, life-altering effects on every stratum of society, from the poor to the privileged. It enlarges the intellect, nourishes creativity, and makes us better citizens (Edmundson, 2004; Hirsch, 2009). A recent Brookings Institution study points to new evidence that affirms the decisive effects of a quality education on individual incomes, lifetime earnings, social mobility, health, and life expectancy. It increases the odds that children will be raised in stable, two-parent families and appreciably decreases the proportion of children raised in poverty. Importantly, the study also confirms that a good education depends, even more than previously thought, on the *effectiveness of the teaching* students receive (Greenstone, et al., 2012).

But alas, most teaching is *not* effective. In the great majority of schools, there are wide, crippling disparities in both what we teach and how well we teach, both within and among schools. In most schools, a dismaying amount of time is spent on nonacademic tasks, with students rarely found reading or writing—arguably the two most educational activities they can engage in. Every credible study (as we'll see in Chapter 2 of this book) confirms these findings.

There is a great, perhaps unprecedented opportunity here for school leaders: multiple studies affirm the fact that improvements in curriculum and instruction depend, more than anything, on effective school and district leadership (Leithwood et al., 2004, in NASSP/NAESP, 2013). If we wanted to, we could ensure that the great majority of our schools *consistently* provide quality curriculum and effective instruction—and reap the immense benefits of doing so. But for this to happen, we must first radically recast the work of school leaders.

It is vital that we *simplify and demystify* school leadership. In 30 years of visiting schools and classrooms, I've become convinced that the primary obstacle to effective leadership is our failure to identify, clarify, and then focus on certain actions that ensure optimal instruction. School leadership has become an unduly profuse, complicated, and *unfocused* business. Administrative training and certification programs have contributed to this complexity: they abound in theories, principles, and approaches, but rarely clarify and equip leaders to execute the most obvious principles and routines that lead to better educational outcomes (Elmore, Evans, & Marshall in Schmoker, 2006). If we want to bring effective instructional leadership within the reach of all school leaders, we must give leaders permission to focus their limited time and energy on the core of good schooling: a widely acknowledged, empirically established set of fairly obvious practices that have the most direct effect on the quality of education.

This book is based on the principles and practices I wrote of in my 2011 book *Focus: Elevating the Essentials to Radically Improve Student Learning,* with a more explicit focus on actions that leadership can take. Though *Leading with Focus* can be read as a companion to *Focus* or on its own, leaders will ideally be familiar with the earlier book and will refer their teachers to it—especially chapters 4–7, which contain detailed information on curriculum and instruction in the core subject areas.

As we'll see in Chapter 1, there is an emerging reverence for the power of simplicity in the workplace. It is critical to effective leadership, productive work, and employee satisfaction. The essence of simplicity is concision and clarity: a tight, near-exclusive focus on the lowest possible number of the most effective and manageable actions and expectations. Simplicity demands that leaders *incessantly* clarify and reinforce these priorities. This book's immodest claim is that focused, straightforward efforts can enable leaders to achieve significant, transformative improvements within one or two school years. The reason for my optimism is that most schools suffer predominantly from certain obvious but crippling shortcomings—namely, a lack of the following three essential elements:

1. A coherent, content-rich curriculum
2. A solid amount of traditional literacy tasks and activities
3. Effective, soundly structured lessons

The power of these three elements has overwhelmingly been established by research—as has the evidence that they are manifestly rare in schools. Once we acknowledge their importance, however, we create an unprecedented opportunity for school or district leaders to have a swift and significant effect on teacher performance and student achievement.

To give you a sense of how powerful the three elements are, consider two very different school districts. School #1 is much like the majority of schools I've visited in dozens of states. Though it's the highest-rated school in a "good" district, I found that *not a single teacher appeared to know how to deliver a nominally effective lesson.* Moreover, every school I visited in the district employed a default curriculum that mostly consisted of short-answer worksheets and excessive amounts of group work. Every year, the district provided schools with a panoply of programs, trainings, and professional development options and initiatives. But there was no attempt—as the central office staff fully conceded—to monitor or refine the implementation of any of these.

School #2 (one of a few that I discuss in detail in Chapter 3 of this book) wasn't perfect. But it was in a district where leadership ensured that all teachers and leaders were thoroughly trained in the basic structure of effective lessons—more specifically, lessons that reflect what virtually every researcher now agrees is central to effective teaching: the teacher's close, ongoing attention to *how many students are succeeding on each step of the lesson*. All teachers in the district were hired—and retained—on the basis of their explicit commitment to mastering and consistently delivering such lessons.

It should be obvious that the stark difference between these two schools is *leadership*. This book is an attempt to explicate and clarify the kinds of straightforward leadership practices employed in School #2. Make no mistake: such practices would enable record numbers of schools to provide high-quality instruction with unprecedented consistency—thus enabling record numbers of students to become knowledgeable, literate, productive citizens. To that end, I've organized the book as follows:

• **Chapter 1** makes the case for simple, focused school leadership, demonstrating the unrivalled power of such an approach for swiftly and substantively improving the quality of work done by both teachers and leaders.

• **Chapter 2** examines the three core elements that I believe should be the focus of leadership efforts in the great majority of schools.

• **Chapter 3** offers examples of schools and districts that have embraced the power of simple, focused school leadership.

• **Chapter 4** provides a flexible implementation guide—a "starter kit" of sorts—for ensuring focused leadership in schools and districts.

Let's now turn our attention to the power of focus for transforming leadership and the quality of our schools.

Focused Leadership: Doing Less—and Doing It Better

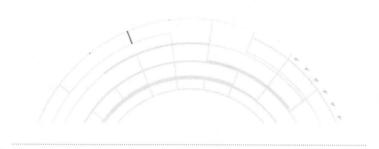

The real path to greatness, it turns out, requires simplicity and diligence. . . . It demands each of us to focus on what is vital—and to eliminate all of the extraneous distractions.

—Jim Collins

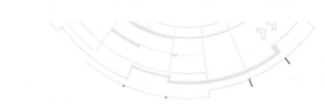

Jim Collins' book *Good to Great* (2001) is the best-selling management book of our generation. At its heart is a profound claim: that ordinary human beings can become exceptional leaders. How? By radically simplifying the work of leadership. To succeed, leaders must carefully select, severely limit, and then persistently clarify (and clarify, and clarify, and clarify) the work to be done by those they lead. They must also reject anything that distracts them from their focus. In short, they must embrace *simplicity*.

An exciting body of research affirms the power of simplicity in any workplace. It is essential to both organizational and personal improvement, and it succeeds because it acknowledges the very real limits of people's time, talent, and concentration. Applied simplicity defines and clarifies precisely what leaders and employees need to focus on—*and what they must be given explicit permission to ignore.* We do our best work when the scope and focus of the work are crystal clear and limited only to what matters most at any given time (Siegel & Etzkorn, 2013; Maeda, 2006).

Focusing on essentials *creates precious time* for us to repeatedly and routinely practice and refine our efforts with minimal distraction or anxiety. When both leaders and employees are given a limited, manageable set of clear priorities or strategies and the opportunity to practice and receive feedback on them, both improvement and enhanced work satisfaction are all but inevitable (Csikszentmihalyi, 1990).

Clear, manageable expectations reduce friction and misunderstandings between leaders and employees. Rather than limit our capacities, they make us more imaginative, productive, and proficient at what we do (Buckingham, 2005). They facilitate execution and allow us to work both faster and smarter. Clear, focused leadership reduces cognitive overload and confusion and makes work easier, more engaging, and pleasurable (Jensen, 2000). It allows us to work with greater confidence and competence. Simplicity promotes consistently high performance, with concomitant results. In our case, that means more teachers who truly know how to teach essential content and skills effectively.

Decades of research by prominent researchers in both education and industry back up the importance of focusing exclusively on a narrow set of priorities (Goodwin, 2011; Buckingham, 2005; Siegel & Etzkorn, 2013; Csikszentmihalyi, 1990; Collins, 2001; Jensen, 2000; Maeda, 2006). To succeed best, leaders must severely limit their focus to the most effective actions and repeatedly—even obsessively—clarify their expectations around those actions. If we can simplify (and, in the process, demystify) effective school leadership, we will multiply the number and proportion of ordinary people who become effective leaders.

"Hedgehog" Focus

Success, Collins tells us, is not the result of complex efforts or innovation, but rather a result of simplicity and diligence applied to an extremely limited set of core concepts or actions. His hero is the single-minded hedgehog of Aesop's fable "The Hedgehog and the Fox." The hedgehog knows well enough to repeat the same simple, ancient practice that always guarantees its safety. Rather than innovate, it does what has always enabled it to thrive: it rolls up into a protective ball. In this way, the hedgehog always triumphs against the complex, unfocused machinations of the fox.

A fairly simple formula emerges from Collins and others whose work focuses on simplicity:

• Carefully determine and severely reduce your focus to the fewest and most manageable priorities,

• Emphatically and repeatedly clarify those priorities throughout your organization, and

- Ensure that everyone stays focused on those priorities and fully commits to them through practice, reflection, and refinement.

To maintain focus, leaders must attain "piercing clarity" regarding their selected priorities and their absolute primacy (Collins, 2005, p. 17). *Clarifying the organization's priorities is the leader's single most important job* (Buckingham, 2005); success is the result of achieving "unbelievable clarity" about what people should focus on and practice (Jensen, 2000, p. 15). As Siegel and Etzkorn put it, "clarity makes for simplicity" (2013, p. 6). Leaders must see that without constant clarification, work will inevitably become more complex. People are easily diverted; an organization's "hedgehog" priorities will only be understood and properly implemented if the leader ceaselessly clarifies which actions do and don't support them.

Leaders, then, must unabashedly explain, illustrate, and advocate for what matters most. And they must just as doggedly clarify what the organization *will not* do: "hedgehog" focus can't be sustained in a climate of distraction, with people's time and attention being pulled in several directions at once. Simplicity "demands each one of us to focus on what is vital and to ignore the rest" (Collins, 2001, p. 91). *That's* simplicity.

If leaders and teachers were to attain piercing clarity about what actions matter most; if we were equally clear about the value and impact of those actions; if we learned and practiced them with "simplicity and diligence" (Collins, 2001, p. 104)—something stunning would happen for our students. To that end, let's examine a small set of leadership actions and principles—a working formula for ensuring the successful implementation of effective elements of good schooling.

A Simple Formula for Effective Leadership

The notion of a "formula" for effective school leadership may sound glib or simplistic—a perversion of simplicity. But as Collins and others demonstrate, there are times when even a fairly simple framework represents our best opportunity to move forward (in Brosnan, 2015).

There are five steps to our formula for effective leadership:

1. Research
2. Reduction
3. Clarification
4. Repeated practice
5. Monitoring

Step 1: Research—Carefully

Leaders' effectiveness depends mightily on what they determine to be what Stephen Covey calls "first things" (Covey, 1989): the best possible actions or practices for their school at a given time. Even if we differ on best practices, it is critical that we make decisions on the basis of good evidence rather than popular appeal. (Alas: schools are not, in the main, evidence-based cultures.) Leaders at every level have traditionally embraced what is popular over what is proven (Corcoran, Fuhrman, & Belcher, 2001; Goodwin, 2011). We see this everywhere. Our bias toward what's popular surely explains our unfounded but steadfast belief in the power of instructional technology (Berliner & Biddle, 1995;

Fullan, 2011; Cuban, 2011). Or consider popular but wholly unproven pedagogic fads, like insisting that students learn best when grouped by ability or "learning style." (These methods have been roundly debunked: see Goodwin, 2011; Willingham, 2009a; Schmoker, 2010.) The vast majority of fads in education are not based on reliable evidence.

Leaders need to make rational, hard-headed choices about what works. Of course, a problem soon emerges: there are many highly effective, proven practices out there. But if we try to do too many of them, our work will "complexify"— and we'll fail. Why? Because, once again, success depends on how much time we can realistically apportion to training and practicing—and training, and practicing—with new methods until everyone has successfully mastered them and made them a habit. This is an iron law of implementation success. But in case you haven't noticed, schools offer an excruciatingly limited amount of time to train and master new practices.

So to succeed, we have to *reduce*.

Step 2: Reduce—Until It Hurts

As John Maeda points out, "The first principle of simplicity is: reduce" (2006, p. 1). Once we have done the research, we must select from among various initiatives on the basis of what is most effective for us right now. I'm reminded of how Steve Jobs would ask his best employees to develop a list of their 100 favorite ideas, then discuss them until they had decided on the best 10. Of those 10, Jobs would choose only 3 for the company to actually work on that year (Isaacson, 2012).

According to Stephen Covey, the most important single leadership principle is *first things first*. Leaders must focus on their highest priorities *before* they attend to anything else. Time devoted to "second" or "third" things is time subtracted from *first* things, which are always starved for time to begin with.

Take the case of curriculum. There is considerable agreement that no method of teaching, however effective, can make up for the absence of a curriculum: a clear guide to what teachers should teach, and the approximate order in which they should teach it, for every course (Darling-Hammond, 2010). No new pedagogy or technology can succeed where the default curriculum consists largely (as too many do) of short-answer worksheets and aimless group activities. In almost every school, there is an urgent need for coherent curriculum; it is a quintessential "first thing." It is foolish to pursue any improvement initiative until work is under way and deadlines are set for completing it.

Success hinges on how much time we can devote to ensuring mastery and successful implementation of any new practice, especially during the early stages. When will we learn that even one new initiative requires far more time for training, practicing, and monitoring than leaders typically allot? This is why Collins, like Maeda, is emphatic on the importance of reduction. His work provides a warning and a promise: don't emulate the fox (whose multiple, complex machinations always fail). Emulate the lowly hedgehog—who executes just one, manifestly proven practice and *always triumphs*.

Severely limiting the number of initiatives you choose to implement isn't easy. It is difficult to maintain a focus on these alone until they are fully implemented and mastered. But this focus enables us to leverage improvement's most precious resource: the time necessary to exhaustively and repeatedly *clarify* and train people in best practices.

In *So Much Reform, So Little Change* (2011), Charles Payne found that our tendency to pursue new initiatives means that there simply isn't enough time for us to accurately convey essential information about any of them. As a result, misunderstandings multiply, implementation fails, and faculty experiences "social demoralization" (p. 30). If we want better schools, we must embrace economy and focus. We must also revere *clarity*—indeed, we must be so clear about our highest priorities that no one could possibly misunderstand or improperly implement our most essential and effective practices.

Step 3: Clarify—Obsessively

If you do nothing else as a leader, be clear.
—Marcus Buckingham

The field of education has not historically made clarity a priority. Surely we know this. We seldom explain, train, and reiterate the most essential practices with sufficient depth and intensity for everyone to achieve at least minimal mastery (Payne, 2011). The cause of clarity hasn't been helped by the fact that our profession routinely traffics in what one observer called "mendacious babble" (Mitchell, 1981, p. viii). Leaders should shun the jargon of academic educationism. Some of our most popular terms never acquired a clear definition in the first place and can thus mean almost anything to anyone (e.g., "metacognition," "balanced literacy," "active learning," "differentiated instruction," "student-centered," "learning styles"). The use of such terms wreaks havoc on the clear communication that is essential to improved practice. Our sloppy imprecision is evident in the tortured formulations of many of the Common Core standards and in our unconscionably muddled, jargon-laced teacher evaluation templates (see Chapters 3 and 4). Lack of clarity is far more consequential than we know. To be effective, schools must develop a clear, common understanding of essential professional terms (DuFour & Marzano, 2011).

An old friend of mine with an extensive business resumé (executive with Procter & Gamble, global head of marketing for Pepsi, chief operating officer of eBay) once told me that the most important early leadership lesson he learned was the need for clarity. He learned the hard way that to bring out the best in employees, leaders must meticulously craft every communication—every goal and directive—and then check with employees to make sure that they properly understood the message. Clarity is essential to productive action.

Perhaps nothing could be more important for educators right now than clarity—about their work, priorities, and practices. For decades, I've seen how average educators aren't sufficiently clear on the most fundamental concepts of schooling (curriculum, literacy, and effective teaching). In the words of management expert Tom Peters,

> communication always sucks. . . . It's the human condition. . . . To make communication even halfway decent, even half the time, you've got to work like hell at it . . . all the time. (quoted in Jensen, 2000, p. 24)

Leaders need to "work like hell" at clear communication. All teachers need and deserve leaders who make strenuous efforts to clearly and continuously communicate the most essential concepts and practices. They need leaders to do this with precision and—just as important— *repetition* (more on this in a moment).

Why haven't most educators mastered the most fundamental elements of good schooling? Because we haven't made clarity a priority. To achieve such clarity, leaders must ensure that someone on their staff explains and teaches and models critical concepts and practices multiple times, with follow-up and reinforcement, probably for the length of teachers' careers. Such focused clarification, modeling, and practice are hardly typical of most professional development, which is typically cursory, shallow, and imprecise. That's because precious time, so essential to achieving "piercing clarity," too often gets shifted to other, ever-newer initiatives. And so our training only leaves traces of true understanding. The result? In the great majority of our schools, students are routinely deprived of the game-changing power of best practices (Odden, 2009; Hirsch, 2009; Marzano, 2007).

The successful schools and districts I describe in this book were exceptionally aware of the critical connection between a reduced, "hedgehog"-style focus and the opportunity for teachers to achieve "piercing clarity" with respect to their priorities. At these schools, it would be difficult for practitioners not to know—or to forget—what was expected of them. But clarity also requires something else: practice. We don't really, deeply understand effective instruction and implementation *until we do it*. Practice—repeated, even "guided" practice, with feedback—is integral to clarity.

Step 4: Practice—Repeatedly

Teaching is a performance art; it requires hands-on training and practice (Pondiscio, 2014). The same is true of properly implementing curriculum and establishing effective literacy practices. We can only attain mastery in our performance of these core elements through repeated practice.

We need plenty of time and multiple opportunities to practice what we learn about the essential components of a good lesson—about how to teach students to analytically read, discuss, and write about various texts. None of the steps involved in mastering these elements is particularly complicated—in fact, they beg to be simplified. But they must be practiced. Repeatedly. Until teachers master their essential moves. This is where operative understanding takes root.

We simply don't engage enough in repeated practice. Institutionally, we never have. Our professional development days, faculty and department meetings must include and be followed by practice sessions as a matter of course. In every training, practitioners need opportunities to actually attempt to employ each major element of a good lesson in small or class-sized groups of their peers—with guidance and feedback—until it is apparent that all have mastered essential practices. If some don't, they need to be given additional time and opportunities to do so.

How important is repeated practice? Consider John Wooden. Perhaps the greatest college basketball coach of all time, he coached UCLA to 10 national championships—7 of them consecutive. Wooden was *obsessed* with repeated practice of basketball fundamentals. His recipe for success was old fashioned and simple. As he put it: "I created eight laws of learning, namely, explanation, demonstration, imitation, repetition, repetition, repetition, repetition, and repetition" (Torbett, 2012, p. 1).

Wooden didn't "innovate"; even his admirers said his approach was from "the 1920s" (Bisheff & Walton, 2004, p. 104). He ceaselessly explained and demonstrated effective practices by having his players repeat fundamentals until they became second nature. Wooden's players didn't just learn—they *overlearned* by repeating best practices "ad nauseam" (p. 104). His players initially resisted—until they came to realize that Wooden's approach had made them world-class players. After college, they found that their overlearning had given them a huge advantage over other players in the NBA.

Leaders should have teachers overlearn best practices, too. Teachers need leaders who aren't bashful about the need to strenuously and repeatedly clarify and provide practice opportunities for teachers to learn and overlearn the fundamentals. We need to train and retrain in the most vital practices until teachers demonstrate mastery—and then periodically retrain again to ensure against forgetfulness and drift. It's because we as a profession haven't embraced the importance of repetition that good practices are still so very rare, even in so-called good schools (Odden, 2009; Marzano, 2007; Elmore, 2000).

The work of leaders like Doug Lemov (author of *Teach Like a Champion*) and Paul Bambrick-Santoyo speaks to the importance of practice. In their "Uncommon Schools" network, Lemov and Bambrick-Santoyo arrange for teachers to learn their craft by being shown, explicitly and repeatedly, how to master a certain teaching method. Then the teachers try the new method on an audience of their peers, during training—and repeat the process until they pass muster.

If we want to turn the corner on making effective practice the new norm, then we must make *repeated, mastery-based practice* the new norm first. Any leader can arrange for this to happen. Repeated practice must become the new model of professional development, of college and university teacher preparation, and of department meetings.

Last, but hardly least: leaders must monitor to ensure school- and districtwide quality and consistency.

Step 5: Monitor—and Respond Immediately

What gets measured and monitored gets done. It should go without saying that leaders must obsess over essential practices and how well they're being implemented. Monitoring should involve a combination of classroom observation, brief meetings, and periodic reviews of data.

Though it's an essential aspect of supervision, monitoring has become a lost art; in most schools, we only pretend to do it. We avoid monitoring because it can often be difficult and unpleasant. We don't yet see that with greater clarity, focus, and repeated practice, monitoring and supervision can become positive experiences for all. Effective supervisory routines are essential and need not be either onerous or time-consuming (as the examples in Chapter 4 will make clear).

Importantly, monitoring should mainly be confined to those aspects of performance that are the most clear, objective, and observable—those areas where teachers have received ample and repeated training and guidance. The trouble begins when we monitor or evaluate for unclear or subjective aspects of teaching. When we evaluate and critique practices that haven't been abundantly and repeatedly clarified, teachers will feel unjustly criticized.

To the greatest extent possible, monitoring should be a positive and productive process. We can ensure this by focusing on practices that teachers have had ample opportunity to learn and rehearse until they reach mastery. Under these conditions, monitoring should mostly consist of capturing and celebrating progress and increased consistency, with plenty of opportunities to compliment practitioners.

Leaders must never make the mistake of thinking that essential practices are so ingrained that they no longer need to be monitored. We've already seen what comes of that mindset—a scarcity of the most critical and highly effective practices in schools.

Focused Leadership

I'll end with a story about a familiar company. I hope it helps to illustrate (if somewhat imperfectly) the principles explored in this chapter: the need to identify and reduce our focus to "first things" based on the best evidence available, to clarify our priorities strenuously, to then practice and repractice to mastery, and to monitor to ensure quality and consistency.

Several years ago, Starbucks president Howard Schultz began an effort to bring the company, which was in a very deep slump, back from the brink of failure. Facing myriad problems, Schultz made a pivotal decision to focus on Starbucks' "first thing": the ability of the average barista to create high-quality espresso on a consistent basis.

As with teaching, there is a lot more to making a high-quality espresso than merely hurrying through the motions. Careful attention must be paid to each step in the process. Starbucks monitors the quality of its espressos, and the company's internal data revealed that both the quality and consistency had dropped precipitously over time. For Schultz, this decline in quality violated "the essence of what we set out to do 40 years ago" (Schultz & Gordon, 2012, p.4).

Against strong advice, Schultz decided to stop for a moment and focus the company's attention—its "hedgehog" focus—on just this one thing. To make clear his commitment, he temporarily shut down every Starbucks coffeehouse in the United States and required every barista to be retrained in the art of making a high-quality espresso. Every single barista received additional training and targeted feedback in this core process. In the short run, Starbucks lost money and some of its market share. But the quality and consistency of espressos began to surge—immediately. The time spent retraining and practicing the core process not only increased the quality and consistency of espresso but also proved to be a "galvanizing event" and the beginning of a stunning turnaround for the company's fortunes (p. 7).

I hope you'll notice that none of the actions Schultz took are particularly complicated. Exceptional leadership requires us to choose the right things to focus on and then devote our ongoing efforts to them with "simplicity and diligence."

In the next chapter, we will more deeply examine the case for the three fundamental elements of effective education—"hedgehog concepts" that we can expect to make a sizeable and immediate difference in the majority of our schools.

Action Steps

Action Step 1: Assess for Focus. All members of the leadership team place a checkmark by the statements below that they believe are currently true for the school or district. If they are not certain about an item, they are to leave it unchecked.

___ We have identified a *severely limited* number of amply proven "hedgehog" practices and expectations for their implementation.

___ We have structures in place for ensuring that every teacher, regardless of experience, is aware of core priorities.

___ Our school leaders reiterate core expectations and connect them to the agenda topics at every faculty meeting.

___ Our leaders know, at any given time, at the *school level,* precisely what practices most require our immediate attention.

___ Our leaders know, at any given time, which *individual teachers or groups of teachers* need additional clarification and practice in core practices.

___ We have built routines into the formal schedule for addressing school and teacher needs immediately, the moment they are identified.

___ We provide frequent, routine opportunities during department and team meetings for teachers to

___ Observe a demonstration lesson by a coach or colleague.

___ Take turns *practicing* selected elements of effective, curriculum-based teaching, with colleagues role-playing as students.

Action Step 2: Plan Focused Action. Members of the leadership team compare their responses to the checklist and reach a group consensus regarding the items on which they need to focus. Of these, leaders should ask: What actions and routines can we implement to ensure simple, clear, repetitious communication, ongoing practice, and effective monitoring of a severely limited number of carefully selected core practices? Leaders then consider current practices that may be stealing precious time from the core priorities they've identified—programs, routines, professional development initiatives, and any other undertakings that distract from the important "hedgehog" practices.

Leadership Opportunities in the Three Key Areas: Curriculum, Literacy, and Instruction

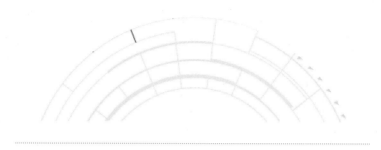

Efficiency is doing things right; effectiveness is doing the right things.

—Peter Drucker

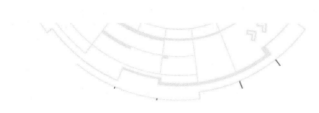

In the last chapter, we saw that the first step toward improvement is identifying, through research and study, a severely limited set of strategic actions that ensure school quality and improvement. The actions that we choose to take are hugely important, as they will determine how faculty members spend thousands of precious hours. These choices should constitute our highest operative priorities. In a smart organization, leaders will continuously clarify, model, practice, and monitor initiatives until all have mastered them.

To this end, it is imperative that priorities are selected on the basis of a careful, objective review of the best available evidence.

In this chapter, I intend to clarify and then make the case for focusing on the following three specific areas:

1. Curriculum,

2. Literacy, and

3. Instruction.

For the great preponderance of our schools, focusing on these three areas will have a stronger effect on school improvement than any other options available to us. Rightly understood, curriculum, literacy, and instruction are grossly underimplemented in the majority of our schools—providing a historic chance for almost any leader to increase the quality and substance of schooling in a relatively short time. To put it differently: when the gap between *best* practices and *common* practices is as wide as it is today in most schools, conditions are optimal for both swift and significant improvement.

To get a sense of this opportunity, consider what happened in the mid-1960s when an enormous shift occurred in the sport of high jumping. Jim Fosbury, a mediocre high jumper, decided one day to try jumping backward—that is, facing away from the high bar as he went over—instead of forward. In an event where progress is measured in fractions of an inch, he was able to make a six-inch gain in *a single afternoon,* having only crudely mastered the new method. All he had to do now was practice, practice, practice. From that day on, coaches everywhere were granted a historic opportunity to improve their athletes' performance almost immediately and by unprecedented margins. Indeed, in the ensuing years, those who adopted the "Fosbury flop" shattered every high jumping record (Burnton, 2012).

Or consider the example of Dr. Atul Gawande and his colleagues, who were able to have stunning and immediate effects on mortality and infection rates in a hospital simply by having staff use simple checklists to ensure that personnel were, for the first time, consistently and correctly implementing best practices in critical areas like hospital hygiene (Henig, 2009). Focusing on simple and effective best practices is the best way to guarantee success no matter the profession, but especially—and, arguably, most important—when it comes to education.

Curriculum

Let's be clear about what we mean by "curriculum." The word refers to those things that are taught *in common* by teachers of the same course in a school or district. It doesn't mean lockstep, air-tight, day-by-day conformity to a scripted program, but rather what most parents already think it means: an adequately defined set of essential topics, concepts, texts, and writing assignments that they can assume the school will provide for their children regardless of which teacher they happen to get. This common curriculum might constitute 60 to 80 percent of the material taught by teachers of the same course.

According to numerous studies, teachers themselves yearn for this type of coherent guaranteed curriculum (Darling-Hammond, 2010; Kauffman, Johnson, Kardos, Liu, & Peske, 2002). It should go without saying that such an approach has to account for the time constraints inherent in a 36-week,

180-day school year. If we try to build too much content into curriculum—a common tendency—it will implode: both content and quality will begin to vary tremendously from teacher to teacher (Marzano, 2003) and drift, inevitably, into "curricular chaos" (Schmoker & Marzano, 1999, p. 17) or "curricular anarchy" (Marshall, 2003, p. 107). In such circumstances, teachers can no longer administer common assessments and the work of professional learning communities becomes impossible (DuFour & Marzano, 2011). In the pages that follow we'll see how to create curriculum that avoids these pitfalls.

The Common-Sense Case for Coherent Curriculum

Before we review the research, let's consider the common-sense case for curriculum. It represents the very substance of an education, of what students will be taught: the essential books and articles they'll read; the topics, concepts, and skills they'll learn; and the amount and types of writing assignments they will complete. A first principle of effective school leadership is that *curriculum matters*—tremendously.

Clear, teacher-friendly curriculum provides focus and allows for both common assessments (which makes things easier for administrators) and meaningful teacher dialogue (which is essential to productive teacher teams). Where there is a common curriculum, teachers aren't left to agonize, in isolation, about which standards they should teach or how much time they should allot to which topics. They no longer must wonder which texts are most essential or helpful for teaching certain topics or guess how many major papers they should assign. The answers to all these questions are provided in the curriculum, which is designed and modified over time by educators at the school or district level.

All teachers deserve a clear and coherent curriculum. It saves them time, lightens their workload, and reduces workplace anxiety and confusion (Kauffman et al., 2002; Anonymous, 2008). Darling-Hammond (2010) goes as far as to say that an approximate guide to what should be taught and when is the still-overlooked but essential *precondition for effective teaching.* My experience and interactions with teachers roundly confirm this. I'm convinced that many of the teachers we may now regard as ineffective could become highly effective if given a decent curriculum to work from on their first day of school.

What the Research Says

A large-scale, systematic analysis of research found that coherent, content-rich curriculum is probably *the single largest factor* affecting levels of achievement in school (Marzano, 2003). By itself, curriculum can alter a school's academic trajectory. Enormous benefits accrue to students who attend a school that can guarantee that certain important, agreed-upon content and literacy skills *are actually taught,* regardless of the teachers they are assigned (Marzano, 2003; DuFour & Marzano, 2011). The research also shows that the acquisition of knowledge and vocabulary through a content-rich curriculum may be more important to reading ability than *any other factor* (Hirsch, 2009; Willingham, 2009b). Small wonder, then, that the call for coherent curriculum has come from a host of prominent researchers and leaders (see, for example, the Spring 2008 issue of the American Federation of Teachers' flagship publication, *The*

American Educator, devoted entirely to the primacy of curriculum to educational improvement).

With so much on the line, we owe it to students—and parents and citizens—to take an honest look at the current state of the actual curriculum that's being taught in the various disciplines. Because curriculum may be the single biggest factor affecting student learning, and because it is patently underimplemented in most schools, there is a tremendous opportunity here for swift, significant improvement.

The Leadership Opportunity

Despite its unparalleled power, decades of studies reveal that guaranteed and viable curriculum continues to be among our lowest operational priorities—it is the rare school or district that provides teachers with a clear, realistic guide to what teachers should teach. In the main, teachers are left to figure curriculum out by themselves.

I've been visiting classrooms in dozens of states for more than 20 years, always in the company of teachers and leaders. In that time and right up to the present, I have consistently witnessed astonishing differences among teachers who teach the same course in the same school. My observations are right in line with the most comprehensive studies—one of which found, for instance, that it wasn't unusual for one teacher to be teaching *27 times* as much science as his or her colleague in the same grade (Berliner, 1984).

Overwhelming majorities of my audiences around the United States confirm that, in the absence of curriculum, students spend more than half of their time in school every day filling out worksheets or engaging in aimless, nonacademic group activities—and it has been this way for decades (Hirsch, 2009). "Curricular chaos" is as prevalent now as it was in the early 1980s, when publication of *A Nation at Risk* set off the United States' latest education reform movement (Dufour & Marzano, 2011; National Commission on Excellence in Education, 1983). Traditional leadership training has been alarmingly indifferent to this "curricular chaos," providing little or no guidance for leaders on how to coordinate the development of curriculum or monitor its implementation.

For teachers, the consequences are predictable. In an anonymously written article for the *American Educator,* one frustrated ex-teacher described her first encounter with the culture of schooling and how shocked she was (as many of us were, as new teachers) by the institutional apathy regarding what she taught. Within a week, it became apparent to her that there was no operative curriculum in her school. All of her queries about what to teach were met with glib indifference. As she put it, the school was more interested in helping her locate the faculty restrooms than it was in what she actually taught her 9th graders. She left teaching after a year and became convinced by her experience that lack of curricular guidance is one of the main reasons so many teachers leave the profession during their first five years (Anonymous, 2008).

And yet, many educators use the word "curriculum," even *"the* curriculum," regularly—*as though its existence and implementation can be assumed.* An insidious force works against us here: the presence of so-called "curriculums" and curriculum documents in every district. Either too scant or too complex, these confusing documents do little to clarify what teachers must teach and when. They do create the *illusion* that there is a curriculum, however, thus preventing us from completing authentic curriculum—a clear, teacher-friendly document that could have as much or more of an influence on learning as any other factor (Marzano, 2003).

The great majority of curriculum guides I've seen are virtually indecipherable. Many are nothing more than barely modified lists of state standards, written in the typically abstract language of their sources and offering no guidance regarding sequence or time allotments. I've sat with numerous assistant superintendents and directors of curriculum and looked at their curriculum guides, and even they will admit that these are pro forma documents, often put together merely for accreditation purposes. (Shame on our accreditation entities!) No one ever "pilots" these documents; no one pays attention to how useful they are for ordinary teachers. Short or long, most are virtually unusable.

I once heard a prominent researcher refer to curriculum guides as "well-intended fictions." Indeed, the very notion that a common curriculum both exists and is actually implemented is a "gravely misleading myth" (Hirsch, 1996, quoted in Marzano, 2003, p. 23). In reality, U.S. public schools have operated in the absence of curriculum for over 60 years (Hirsch, 2009). It's long past time we introduced this hugely powerful factor into schools where it currently has barely a foothold. Any leader who prioritizes coherent common curriculum will reap immense benefits, most likely starting in the very first year of implementation.

And what of literacy—an integral element of curriculum itself? Is there a similarly rich opportunity for improvement here as well? Teachers would do well to ask: In the course of one six-hour school day, *what* and *how much* do students *actually read*? How much do they *write*, and *what do they write about*? As you're about to find out, the answers to these questions are quite disturbing—but they point to the opportunity for leaders to achieve exceptional results through fairly simple, straightforward actions.

Authentic Literacy

Again, and as with "curriculum": we must be very clear about what we mean by "literacy." The word has been tortured by modernists who would have it mean almost anything but what it was originally intended to mean: the ability, first and foremost, to effectively read, talk, and write about a wide variety of sufficiently complex, high-quality literature and nonfiction. Literacy includes the ability to read, discuss, and write in the analytical, explanatory, and especially argumentative mode in every course, including electives and the arts. It also includes a manifest ability to write both short- and long-form essays, proposals, and research papers—skills invaluable in both the academy and the workplace. The acquisition of literacy, thus defined, is the primary means of acquiring knowledge, thinking skills, and verbal facility.

Amid the confusion and controversy surrounding English language arts (ELA) standards, it is easy to lose sight of the fairly simple definition of literacy outlined above. I largely endorse the general emphasis that the Common Core standards place on wide reading and more writing across the curriculum, on close reading of high-quality text, and on argument as the primary mode of reading, writing, and discussion. To that I say: Bravo. But the grade-by-grade standards are a different matter—they are still too numerous and confusing. A former president of the Modern Language Association found most of them to be hopelessly ambiguous and unnecessary (Schmoker & Graff, 2011). One prominent curriculum expert went as far as to call them "just another set of blithering, poorly thought-out abstractions" (Shepherd in Ravitch, 2013).

I have to agree. For this reason, I believe it is critical for leaders to reacquaint themselves and their school faculties with the traditional definition of literacy. It is increasingly apparent that a focus on the simple core elements of literacy every year would satisfy the demands of any standards-based test while at the same time truly preparing students for college and careers. I therefore welcome the recent release of the clear and concise "three shifts" on which the Common Core architects themselves are now telling us to concentrate our literacy efforts:

1. Building knowledge through content-rich nonfiction;
2. Reading, writing, and speaking grounded in evidence from texts, both literary and informational; and
3. Regular practice with complex text and its academic language.

Once students can decode, these three elements represent a simple and clear definition of literacy—*for all grade levels*—with which teachers and leaders can begin their work.

What the Research Says

Purposeful reading, writing, and discussion are integral to quality curriculum—in fact, they constitute the primary means of becoming educated (Rose, 1989; Lasch, 1995). This reality remains true even in our technology-obsessed age. As Thomas Friedman writes, the primary skill set for success in the 21st century is advanced proficiency in "plain old reading and writing" (2005, p. 353). Those who are truly literate and articulate "will rise to the top of the pack" (Gardner, 2009, p. 18).

Just as knowledge is integral to reading and comprehension, so too is the acquisition of academic literacy. As Hirsch (2010) puts it, literacy is "the most important single goal of schooling in any nation" because it both requires and further enables the acquisition of knowledge (p. 31). In fact, a recent and exhaustive study by David Conley and colleagues reveals that levels of literacy account more than anything for success in college, with the ability to read and write in the academic mode being perhaps the single most important predictor of college success (2007, p. 27). If you graduate from high school able to write research papers in serviceable academic prose, you are prepared to succeed at most four-year colleges. Another study found that both achievement gaps and earnings gaps between racial and ethnic groups in the United States *largely disappear* when language competence is factored into the equation (Hirsch, 2009, p. 31). Conversely, research shows that a lack of verbal competence in reading, speaking, and writing is the primary reason students drop out of high school and college (Ferrandino & Tirozzi, 2004).

The Leadership Opportunity

The fact that we must make the case for something as fundamental to education as literacy points to how grossly we misunderstand what it means to be educated. Nonetheless, the case must be made. Our failure to appreciate the immense importance of traditional literacy becomes especially apparent when we take an honest look at how time is allotted in the average school day: by any reckoning, authentic literacy is among the lowest priorities in schools. In a typical six-hour school day, students actually *read* for only a few minutes—and if they are poor readers or in special education, even less than that (Schmoker, 2006, pp. 76–77). According to one source, "There is no reading in the reading curriculum. . . . Children read for a remarkably small percentage of the school day" (Calkins, Montgomery, & Santman, 1998, pp. 51–52). Moreover, the quality and density of the texts students read have declined precipitously. Students too often are asked to read texts that are easier *by several grade levels* than those students read in the 1970s (Stotsky, 1999). As writing expert Donald Graves points out, most teachers don't actually teach writing, they merely assign it (in Jones, 1995, p. 23).

These grim realities are almost as true of high-scoring schools as they are of low-scoring ones. My daughters attended a high-scoring school in which only two or three novels were assigned each year in English classes. One of the principals at the school even admitted that not a single English teacher actually taught writing or even assigned any essays of even a few pages in length. In one class—Honors English—students only wrote poems and performed skits. Even so, the school was ranked among the top 100 charter schools in the country by *U.S. News and World Report.*

In her 2010 book *The Flat World and Education,* Linda Darling-Hammond cites a trenchant passage from one of Tom Wolfe's best-selling novels. A parent called the high school to see how his son was doing, specifically on "written work." The principal "let out a whoop" and then said,

> Written work? There hasn't been any written work at Rupert High for fifteen years! Maybe twenty! They take multiple choice tests. Reading comprehension. That's the big thing. That's all the Board of Education cares about (Wolfe, 1987, pp. 130–31).

Darling-Hammond goes on to review some of the currently accepted notions of what students should do after reading a text or novel. For example, instead of discussing or writing about the text, she notes that students are often asked to make projects or movies or artifacts out of toothpicks or clay (2010). That such activities crowd out authentic, college- and career-oriented literacy activities can no longer be disputed. Cheryl Sandberg, chief operating officer for Facebook, recently lamented that she wrote only a single five-page paper in high school, then "had to write five-page papers overnight" in college (Alter, 2014, p. 72).

There's a word for these frighteningly common traditions in our schools: *malpractice.*

Leaders: you don't come across opportunities like this very often. You will rarely find so egregious a gap between best practice and common practice. To make a difference, you don't need to be a literacy expert; you simply need to take the most obvious and immediate actions to transform the quality of schooling students receive. If you want to make a mark as a school leader—if you want to prepare record numbers of students for the rigors of college, careers, and informed citizenship—simply ensure that teachers do the following:

• Build a liberal number of specific, common readings into their respective course curriculums, including at least eight whole books in English per year, at least one book per year in social studies or history, and greatly increased levels of text-based instruction—especially in English, social studies, and science. (For explicit guidance, see chapters 4–7 in *Focus*.)

• Scaffold all reading assignments so that challenging texts are accessible to all students: teach critical vocabulary, provide purpose and background for every text, and model and explicitly instruct students in the kinds of critical reading you expect them to do in every subject (see *Focus*, pp. 74–89).

• Teach students *how to underline and annotate* important points as they read to argue, interpret, or explain and to consult their notes as they participate in discussions and write nonfiction papers.

• Provide systematic, step-by-step instruction on how to produce both short, informal papers and long, formal research papers—and insist on specifications in every course for the *number and length of writing assignments* that are to be taught.

• Gradually increase the proportion of essay tests.

• Collect and codify student and professional examples of good writing.

Leaders must ensure that the above activities are among the highest priorities for teachers, who can immediately begin helping students to read, talk, and write across the curriculum. Don't let anyone tell you that this is rocket science: any honest, collective effort by teachers and teams to fulfill these activities will yield good results while also satisfying the demands of ELA standards.

Once again: What would happen to current levels of achievement, graduation rates, and college success rates if leaders began to give due focus to this quintessential aspect of schooling and curriculum? How much more articulate, well-read, and able to think critically would students be if a traditional conception of literacy regained its proper place in the school day?

As fundamental as curriculum and literacy are to sound schooling, there is one other obvious element that could have an equally profound effect: soundly structured instruction, on which the most effective delivery of literacy-rich curriculum depends. (Please indulge me here: the following section requires slightly more substantial treatment.)

Effective Instruction

For decades, we have known the proven rudiments of effective lessons across the subject areas. Excellent work has been done to codify and formalize these core elements in a way that allows teachers to understand and apply them with almost immediate success (as was the case for me personally). A legion of our best researchers now agree on the basic features of a good lesson—and on just how game-changing good lessons can be (Hattie 2009; Marzano, 2007; Popham, 2008; Wiliam, 2007).

In most cases, effective instruction begins with a clearly written *learning objective* or *target* that establishes the purpose for the lesson and how the lesson will be assessed. ("Plate tectonics" is not an objective; "I can describe the three most essential components of plate tectonics in writing" is.) For many lessons, a rich, text-based question to be answered in discussion or writing can serve as a learning objective.

The most effective lessons are taught in carefully sequenced steps, or "chunks." It is imperative for teachers to check for understanding between each chunk of a lesson. If students aren't grasping the content, teachers must adjust instruction to ensure the success of as many students as possible. The ultimate goal is for every student to be able to succeed at each stage of instruction and, eventually, on an assessment of the lesson. This approach is known as "gradual release of responsibility" (Pearson & Gallagher, 1983). The teacher assumes primary responsibility for ensuring that all students understand each chunk of the lesson until they are able to assume "responsibility" for the lesson—that is, to successfully complete each step without the teacher's help.

Clear learning objectives, step-by-step teaching, focused practice, checking for understanding, and adjusting of instruction are the most important elements of effective lesson delivery. Without these elements, students who struggle early on in a lesson will fall further behind with each subsequent step. These basic moves are fundamental to all instruction, including the most intellectually rigorous academic work.

On some level, we all know that these elements are important. But here's the thing: we can't expect lessons that embrace these elements to become the norm until leaders understand and communicate their outsize importance and are able to adequately execute sound lessons themselves. The elements of effective instruction apply to all lessons; for Robert Marzano, they should be "routine components" of effective teaching *for every lesson in every subject* (Marzano, 2007, p. 180).

I would emphasize that good lessons do not have to be particularly "creative"; they don't depend on exceptional talent or skill. In fact, studies of the best schools show that their lessons are surprisingly ordinary—"plain vanilla" (Goodwin, 2011, p. 135). As Coach Wooden found, real creativity thrives within a culture where people have mastered fundamentals (Bisheff & Walton, 2004).

We underestimate the need for leaders to understand and be able to explain, demonstrate, and evaluate the most critical core processes of the work being done by those they lead. Ideally, mastery of these core processes would be a prerequisite for all leadership positions (Pfeffer & Sutton, 2000). To that end, I encourage you to carefully examine and discuss the elements in Figure 2.1, which I refined over time with the help of several teachers and leaders. I hope that you can use this figure as a quick-reference tool. (For a more detailed discussion of the elements for use in training, coaching, and assessment, see Appendix A.)

What the Research Says

• According to Popham (2008), the effects of these essential elements on student learning are "among the largest ever recorded" (p. 2).

• Hattie (2009) notes that *hundreds of studies* confirm the immense value of each respective essential element.

• Wiliam (2007) points out that the elements have served as the basis for the most effective teaching over *millennia;*

2.1 The Elements of Effective Lessons

One hundred percent of students should be attentive and engaged throughout every lesson, which should consist of the following elements:

Clear Learning Objective	The objective is PROMINENTLY posted and based on grade level curriculum—and written in crystal clear language. The objective includes—or leaves no doubt about—how the learning will be demonstrated/assessed. Teacher refers/points to the objective throughout the lesson.
Anticipatory Set	Teacher provides preview/background/purpose for lesson: to motivate, connect, provoke curiosity (3–5 minutes maximum); may include embedded vocabulary from text(s) to be used in lesson.
Teaching & Modeling	Teacher clearly teaches/models/"thinks aloud" for each component of lesson—one brief, manageable step/chunk at a time. (Teacher is always "scanning" while teaching: to ensure that all eyes are on the teacher during modeling.) Each brief step must be immediately followed by "guided practice.". . .
Guided Practice	After each brief step/chunk in the lesson, the teacher immediately gives students a chance to practice/process information and to demonstrate understanding or mastery of that brief step that was just taught or modeled, while the teacher "checks for understanding.". . .

Checking for Understanding	Both during and after each "guided practice," for every small step/chunk in the lesson, the teacher uses strategies to check for understanding—that is, to quickly assess students' progress or mastery (e.g., by circulating to observe students' work/answers; cold-calling a random sample of students; having students hold up whiteboards with work/answers). (The teacher does little/no individual "tutoring" during this time, which interrupts the flow of the lesson and is less efficient than the next step—adjusting instruction [below] for the entire class. Tutoring can be done during "independent practice.") --- The information gathered during each guided practice/check for understanding is used to inform the teacher's attempt to adjust instruction, that is, to reteach clarify a portion of instruction until students are ready to move on to the next step.
followed by **Adjustments to Instruction**	
Independent Practice	The above cycle is repeated, sometimes multiple times, for every step in the lesson—until virtually all students are ready for "independent practice": to complete the day's assignment/assessment of the objective on their own. If necessary, tutoring/small group assistance can be provided to those needing additional help at this time.

that if all U.S. teachers used the basic elements of sound instruction, the United States would move into the top five in math performance internationally; that the elements allow teachers to cover *up to four times* as much curriculum when compared to the most common current teaching approaches; that they would add six to nine months of growth *per year* for the average student; and that it is *more than 20 times as effective* as the most popular pedagogic fads and initiatives—and would have *10 times as much* of an effect as reductions in class size.

• Marzano (2007) strongly recommends that the basic elements be considered "routine components" of every lesson in every subject area (p. 180).

• According to Ripley (2010), teaching based on the elements was the primary factor accounting for the success of the highest-performing teachers in the Teach for America program.

I can personally attest to how relatively easy it can be to learn the elements of effective instruction and deliver lessons that embrace them. At one of the schools where I worked, it took me about two weeks to learn and then successfully implement the elements of sound instruction. The effect on my teaching was immediate and powerful: even my crude understanding of the elements allowed me to teach at least twice as many students as I previously had in any given lesson—and in much less time. (A similar example: In a recent *Edutopia* article, a teacher describes how checking for understanding and adjusting instruction allows her to ensure student mastery of content in three days instead of the usual five, with almost no time spent tutoring [Davis, 2015].)

I consider the use of sound lessons to be a civil rights issue, in that such lessons reflect an active, organized concern for *all* students, including those who struggle. When we ensure that all teachers master and implement effective lessons, we are sending a strong, simple message: that we care enough about every single individual who might need additional clarification or encouragement. We want to know how well students are learning long before the lesson is over so that we can do all in our power to help them succeed in every lesson, every day.

And yet, the evidence is depressingly clear: effective teaching is dismayingly rare in our classrooms—a reality that only makes the opportunity for leaders all the more profound.

The Leadership Opportunity

Ours is a propitious moment for any leader intent on improving the quality of instruction in a school or district. When it comes to effective instruction, there is almost nowhere to go but up. I have observed classrooms in countless schools, and I am consistently struck by the absence of soundly structured lessons. Rarely do I see clear, prominently posted, student-friendly learning objectives; scaffolded instruction explicitly aimed at ensuring success on end-of-lesson assessments; students engaged in guided practice; or teachers conducting checks for understanding. What I *do* see are teachers *routinely calling on students with their hands raised*—a dead giveaway that teachers don't understand the essence of a good lesson. Most lessons I've observed consist of a brief period of instruction or directions (usually ignoring the most critical elements) followed by worksheet assignments or aimless, inordinately extended group activities.

Far too often, large numbers of students are visibly inattentive or disengaged for much of the lesson.

I'm certainly not alone in making these observations:

• Author and educator Eleanor Dougherty and her colleagues found that, instead of being taught explicitly how to perform legitimate academic tasks, students spend most of their time filling in worksheets, coloring maps, creating book covers, and making posters—at all grade levels (2012, p. 8).

• Jay Mathews, longtime education writer for the *Washington Post*, has observed that "the thing that hinders so many [teachers] . . . is that they rush through lessons too fast without stopping long enough to see *whether everyone—or anyone—understands* (my emphasis; 2015, p. 1).

• Over 10 years and in 5,000 classroom visits, author and educator Barry Beers has found that less than 5 percent of teachers employed checks for understanding, communicated clear learning objectives, or engaged in activities visibly connected to the completion of a clear learning objective (Beers, n.d.).

• According to Stanford historians of education David Tyack and Larry Cuban, effective practices "never take root in more than a small proportion of classrooms and schools" (in Elmore, 2000, p. 6).

This has to change. Any leaders willing to set aside less important initiatives can train and retrain teachers in the vital components of effective instruction—modeling, repeating, and reviewing the elements of good lessons at every possible occasion. We must begin to hire teachers on the basis of commitment to the elements of sound lessons.

Ripe for Leadership: A Story of Two Young Ladies at Starbucks

In the three key areas of focus—curriculum, literacy, and instruction—leaders have an exceptional opportunity to make a marked difference in teacher practice and, by extension, student achievement. To get a vivid sense of the effect that leadership actions might have, let me close this chapter with a story from the perspective of students: two young high school girls I met in a local coffee shop.

The first thing I asked the two girls was what and how many books they had to read that year. At first their faces went blank; then one of the girls told me they had read *To Kill a Mockingbird*. The girls admitted to me that many students never actually read the book—but they did see the movie in class, which consumed most of a week's instructional time. When I asked how they had been asked to study the book, one of them reached into her English folder.

There it was: the ubiquitous multi-page worksheet. It contained dozens of mostly lower-order questions about the novel, with less than an inch of space provided for each answer. I've been seeing these for years; my own daughters regularly received packets of them as "study guides." And like my daughters, these two girls were given an entire week of class time—five instructional days—to go through the book in groups (of course) and answer each question (when, in practice, they chatted and borrowed answers from each other). This group work amounted to the only "writing" students were asked to do on the subject of Harper Lee's immortal novel.

I asked the girls more generally about writing in school. They told me they had written "a few essays" that year. One of the girls showed me what she said was a typical "essay": a half-page, two-paragraph piece with a single comment and letter grade at the top. I gathered that these students never wrote anything resembling a college writing assignment.

Thinking back on other lessons over the year, the girls shared with me that they had read (only) a summary of Homer's *Odyssey* and then watched a movie based on it. The movie? The Coen brothers' comedy *O Brother, Where Art Thou?*—an extremely loose retelling of the story set in the Depression-era South. Five days were devoted to viewing the movie. The students never actually read or discussed Homer's original work. (Nor, for that matter, did they write anything about the movie.)

How typical is this scenario? I can only say that I see similar practices in the great majority of schools in every state I visit—even in the so-called "good" schools. In fact, the girls at Starbucks were enrolled in Honors English at the *most prestigious high school* in the area, with high test scores and an A-plus rating from the state. The school district had spent years in a regional Common Core consortium and devoted countless hours to planning how to implement the standards. But none of this busy work protected these students, or tens of millions of others like them, from the ravages of what Michael Fullan so rightly called "the awful inertia of past decades" (2005, p. 33).

Getting Teachers On Board for Change

Although the status quo may sound grim, it also provides a tremendous leadership opportunity. As Carl Glickman (2002) has aptly noted, "school improvement is not a mystery" (p. 4). On the contrary, it has always been about something rarely learned in administrative training: *a willingness to attend methodically and exclusively to very obvious, fundamental elements of schooling.* This doesn't require extra time or money. School leaders could change the landscape of U.S. education simply by ensuring that

• A clear, useful, teacher-friendly curriculum exists for every course.

• Every teacher is given every opportunity to master the simple, intuitive moves associated with a traditional conception of literacy (i.e., purposeful reading, discussion, and writing about lots of rich, challenging texts).

• Every teacher learns—from day one and with frequent repetition and reinforcement—how to master the elements of good lessons.

These should be all school leaders' three highest, near-exclusive "hedgehog" priorities—and leaders should remind teachers of *why* they are so important. As Daniel Pink (2009) reminds us, knowing what to do isn't enough; people need to also know *why it's worth doing.* If teachers are going to accept change, they need to understand that we are asking them to change for the better. Teachers need and deserve to know that focusing on these three key elements of sound instruction will probably have greater benefits for their students than anything else they do. The evidence demands that educators drop whatever interferes with the three key elements; perhaps hardest of all, we must be willing to ignore the continuous wave of distractions that divert time and energy from our highest priorities. As management expert Peter Block (1999) tells us, *we must stop providing people with additional training until they have truly mastered the most fundamental practices necessary to their success.* Because the real problem is not that we don't know what to do; it is that we don't do what we already know.

In the next chapter, we'll see how several schools and districts demonstrate the power of the core elements of effective instruction. More importantly, we'll see how their simple systems demystify school leadership and how they reveal that ordinary actions can lead to exceptional results (beyond just test scores). In Chapter 4, you'll find detailed, step-by-step guidance on how to implement the three core elements successfully.

Action Steps

Action Step 1: Assess for Focus. All members of the leadership team place a checkmark by the statements below that they believe are currently true for the school or district. If they are not certain about an item, they are to leave it unchecked.

Curriculum

___ We have a simple, content-rich curriculum in place for every course that all teachers can easily read, understand, and implement with confidence.

___ The curriculum designates the core topics and skills that should be taught on a weekly or biweekly basis (with some room left for teacher discretion).

___ All teachers consistently implement the curriculum.

Literacy

___ The curriculum includes a generous number of agreed-upon texts in all content areas that are aligned with selected topics and concepts outlined in the curriculum.

___ Students routinely read, discuss, and write about the texts included in the curriculum during the school day.

Instruction

All teachers:

___ fully understand,

___ routinely practice, and

___ consistently implement the major components of effective instruction.

Action Step 2: Plan Focused Action. Given what you now know about the three key areas of schooling, consider the unchecked items in Action Step 1. As a leadership team, discuss your assessment and plan of action with the following questions in mind:

• Do the unchecked items fall predominantly in one or two of the key areas, or in all three?

• How would you prioritize the unchecked items in terms of their likely overall effect on students? In what order would you tackle their implementation?

• What obstacles will you need to surmount in order to address the unchecked items?

3

Focused Leadership
in Action: Examples
from Schools and Districts

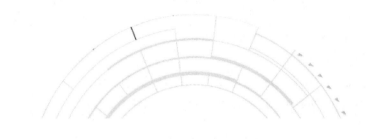

Leaders are well advised to spend 10 times as much energy on the change they just made than looking for the next great change to try.

—Kenneth Blanchard

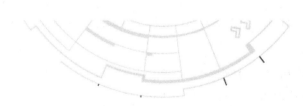

None of the schools and districts in this chapter is perfect. I don't know that any of them fully implemented focused, sound practice in all three of the key areas of curriculum, literacy, and instruction. Indeed, all have something to learn from each other. Even so, each school reveals the power of clarity, redundancy, and simplicity by focusing on one or more of the three fundamental elements discussed here *to the exclusion of most everything else.* All of the schools demonstrate the power of the most simple but effective forms of monitoring and supervision, and all of them reflect an abiding *obsession with consistency*—that is, with ensuring that every teacher actually implements best practices on a routine basis. Taken together, the following schools point to a ripe opportunity for ordinary teachers and administrators to become highly effective leaders.

Example 1: Brockton High School: Focus on a Literacy-Rich Curriculum

Susan Szachowicz was a teacher and department head at the largest high school in Massachusetts: Brockton High, with a student population of more than 4,000. When Szachowicz worked there, Brockton was also among the most disadvantaged and lowest achieving high schools in the state. Appalled—but emboldened—by these results, school administrators gave Szachowicz and her leadership team the opportunity to implement a simple but radical plan to

1. Establish a clear, sequential curriculum for every course and a weekly schedule for teaching the most essential topics from the state assessment, with an emphasis on reading, writing, speaking, and reasoning. (In fact, "reading, writing, speaking, and reasoning" would soon become the team's mantra.)

2. Incorporate writing into most lessons according to a weekly or monthly schedule.

3. Train teachers to teach according to the principles of effective lessons outlined in Chapter 2 (and common to all of the schools described in these pages). At every professional development session and faculty meeting, the leadership asked teachers to (in Szachowicz's words) "practice, practice, practice" the fundamental

elements of two key focus areas: literacy and effective instruction.

4. "Monitor like crazy" (again, in Szachowicz's words): building leaders conducted frequent, unannounced classroom visits to provide continuous feedback and support for the two key areas of focus. All teachers knew they would be evaluated on the basis of their commitment to the focus areas.

5. Train and empower department heads to serve as key leaders in the improvement process.

The simplicity of the team's plan allowed leaders and teachers to stay focused and to monitor implementation effectively: everyone was perfectly clear on what to look for and expect. Susan even referred to the elements of the plan as "hedgehog" concepts.

The first year of implementing the plan was difficult, with some faculty members resisting any change in procedures. But the early results were stunning. When I visited Szachowicz in her office in Brockton, she recounted an important call she received after the first year from David Driscoll, the state commissioner of education. He informed her that Brockton High had made the largest gains in the state.

The school's unswerving focus on fundamental, proven practices had had an immediate and dramatic effect. The plan's success was the result of collaborative efforts by a leadership team comprising teacher leaders and department heads. When any single team member spoke on behalf of the initiative, staff knew that he or she represented a unified team with a deep commitment to Brockton's underserved students. All leaders should avail themselves of school-based leadership teams, which offer many advantages (especially in the early stages).

And Brockton's success didn't stop after the first year: Over the next 10 years, achievement levels and state ranking continued to rise—in a state with arguably the most challenging standards and assessments in the country. Brockton climbed from the very bottom into the state's top 10 percent. Eventually, the school would have the state's highest proportion of minority students receiving the prestigious Adams college scholarship—earned on the basis of high state assessment scores. Brockton's success drew national attention: the story of its dramatic turnaround was featured on the front page of the *New York Times* (Dillon, 2010).

In time, the school was held up as a model of what can happen when leaders eschew instructional fads and instead focus on—and *only* on—the most critical elements of curriculum, literacy, and instruction. Susan was emphatic in pointing out that the leadership at Brockton High achieved its success without "differentiating" students into groups by ability, culture, or preferred "learning styles" and without spending *a single additional dollar.*

The story of Brockton High School attests to the power of a simple, ferocious focus on the fundamentals of school success, reinforced through frequent, deep, intensive efforts to clarify, practice, and monitor their implementation. And when the going gets tough—as it will—successful leadership teams don't retreat: they close ranks and reiterate why they are doing what they are doing. All leaders should be humble enough to make adjustments when criticism or resistance warrants sensible changes. They should also always be clear and repetitive about what they expect from staff.

Example 2: Mather Elementary School: Gains Made with "Amazing Speed"

Mather Elementary School was a low-performing, mostly minority public elementary school in Boston. For years, principal Kim Marshall attempted to arrest what he called the "curricular anarchy" that prevails in the majority of U.S. schools: the fact that teachers of the same course don't tend to stick to an approximately common set of topics and standards. Persistent and courageous, Marshall eventually convinced his teachers to create a curriculum based on the most essential state standards, with a heavy emphasis on purposeful reading and writing. As he put it to me in an e-mail:

> When the [Massachusetts Comprehensive Assessment System] became real—that is, when we got the word that our elementary students wouldn't get a high school diploma if they didn't pass the rigorous 10th grade test—we got hold of the 4th and 8th grade standards (the only grades with standards at that point) and sample assessment items and teased out the most essential standards for grades 3, 2, 1, and kindergarten and then up to grade 5. We then produced compact booklets of curricular expectations for each grade level, with sample reading passages and student writing exemplars, and printed copies for all staff and parents.

Put simply: *the leadership team clarified the curriculum.* And Marshall began to make frequent visits to classrooms to ensure that the curriculum was being faithfully taught. He then arranged for teachers to meet regularly in grade-level teams to help each other develop effective lessons aligned directly with the essential standards.

In Marshall's words, his school's focus on curriculum, collaboration, and frequent monitoring raised achievement levels "with amazing speed" (Marshall, 2003, p. 112). As was the case at Brockton High, some of the largest gains at Mather came in the first year, when scores rose from the bottom to the top third in citywide standings—the greatest gains of any large elementary school in Massachusetts.

Such is the power of a systematic if imperfect effort to move toward a "guaranteed and viable curriculum"—perhaps the single largest factor that affects school achievement (Marzano, 2003, p. 22).

Example 3: Adlai Stevenson High School: A Single-Minded Focus on Curriculum

Let's now look at a school I've written about several times over the years: Adlai Stevenson High School in Lincolnshire, Illinois. It was already a successful school when principal Rick DuFour famously implemented a plan to raise achievement even more. The school's success demonstrates the role that course-alike teacher teams can and should play in the development and consistent delivery of coherent curriculum taught on a roughly common schedule. Once the fundamentals are in place, such professional learning teams play a leading role in reinforcing and refining the quality of both curriculum and instruction over time.

At Stevenson, departments and course-alike teams took the lead on curriculum. Improvement efforts began with a charge to severely reduce the number of standards that teachers taught in each course. This mandate became the basis for constructing a common curriculum and *curriculum-based* assessments for every course and grading period, taught on a common but not overly restrictive schedule (about 15 percent of each course was left to teacher's discretion). The clear, common curriculum and assessments were essential to each team's collective focus and a boon to productive, improvement-oriented collaboration. Once the curriculums were completed, teams continued to meet on a regular basis to improve the effectiveness of their daily lessons—work that can only occur where a common curriculum is in place.

One of the primary reasons for Stevenson's success was a brief, focused quarterly review of each course-alike team's performance. The work was distributed among the principal, assistant principals, and department heads (who were true subject-area leaders). At those meetings, leaders asked simple, common-sense questions: How well did students in each respective course perform that quarter? Was performance even somewhat higher than last quarter? If not, what could leaders do to improve performance in the coming quarter?

Moreover, Stevenson embraced the same model of effective instruction discussed in Chapter 2. Tim Kanold, DuFour's assistant principal and successor as principal and superintendent, noted that his primary objective when conducting classroom observations was to promote purposeful, curriculum-based lessons that featured chunked lessons, guided practice, and checks for understanding—for each step of instruction. Kanold was especially emphatic about the importance of checking for understanding and circulating around the classroom during student guided practice: for him, such "real-time, same-day" assessments of progress are the heart of effective lessons (see *Focus*, p. 66). After conducting his walkthroughs, Kanold would report his findings to the relevant departments or at faculty meetings with a clear expectation for targeted improvements. Kanold, who now writes and consults nationally, has found that very few schools actually teach in this fashion.

Adlai Stevenson's efforts paid off handsomely. The school became one of the most celebrated education success stories of the last generation, making continuous gains for several years on every in-house, curriculum-based assessment as well as on state and college entrance exams. Between 1990 and 2013, the school's median ACT scores rose from 22 to 26.5—even as the state began to require all students, including the non-college-bound, to take the test. During this same period, the school achieved an *800 percent* increase in the number of students passing AP exams (DuFour, 2014).

The leadership at Stevenson accomplished all of this with a deep, intensive focus: DuFour was emphatic that during the first five years of the improvement effort Stevenson conducted no additional or external professional development whatsoever—and, like Brockton, without any additional expenditures.

Now let's examine in depth a district that offers among the best examples of simple, focused leadership that I have come across.

Example 4: Flowing Wells K–12: A Ferocious Focus on Effective Lessons

Flowing Wells Unified School District serves a lower-middle-class community in Tucson, Arizona. I became acquainted with Flowing Wells while working in a neighboring school and taking a graduate course taught by the district's long-time superintendent, Robert Hendricks. As his district racked up accomplishments, I was increasingly struck by the stark differences between Flowing Wells and the district in which I was working. Those differences allowed Flowing Wells to accomplish something truly rare among districts: ensuring that virtually every teacher in every school provided soundly structured lessons almost every period, every day.

In the late 1980s and '90s, student achievement scores at Flowing Wells perennially ranked among the highest in Arizona. Every one of the district's five schools was honored as among the top schools in either the state or nation; twice, the district high school was honored as one of the best in the United States. In 1989, Hendricks was named Arizona Superintendent of the Year (Copenhaver, 1996). The leadership at Flowing Wells had created a legacy: many years after Hendricks's retirement, district schools continued to rank among the state's highest achieving schools.

And for what it's worth: I once heard author and consultant Harry Wong tell an audience that Flowing Wells was perhaps the most effective school district he had ever seen.

So: What was their secret?

Communicating a Common Limited Focus

In the district next to Flowing Wells where I worked, our agenda and priorities were typical of most aspiring, cutting-edge districts. We had an extravagantly funded and amply staffed technology department. We took pride in our extensive menu of programs, methods, and training options in every then-popular teaching technique. And—like most districts—we wholly embraced the time-consuming process of "strategic planning": we would spend days formulating mission statements, conducting needs assessments, administering surveys, and developing elaborate "action plans" for each of our dozens of improvement goals and initiatives. For all of this, we never achieved anything like districtwide consistency in the quality of instruction students received.

Leaders at Flowing Wells spent time and money quite differently. As Hendricks informed me—in words I won't forget—they "weren't enamored of trends." The district did not offer a series of workshops with a menu of various staff development options.

District leaders also dismissed the idea of technology as a primary driver of improvement and consciously shunned the popular but unproven machinations of "strategic plans," which have been found to have little or no effect on actual performance (Mintzberg, 1994, as cited in Schmoker, 2004).

Instead, like the organizations in *Good to Great* (Collins, 2001), the Flowing Wells leadership team combed through the evidence to determine what *single initiative* would have the biggest possible effect on student learning. As Hendricks told me, "People deserve to work in a system that is research-driven, research-proven."

On the basis of the evidence, the team concluded that the consistent delivery of soundly structured lessons would become Flowing Wells' "hedgehog" concept. The district would focus on ensuring that every teacher had fully mastered and was consistently implementing effective lessons every day and in every class period. "We kept it simple," Hendricks told me. The result? Scores rose and the accolades came rolling in.

So, how did the leadership team at Flowing Wells make sure that every teacher taught soundly structured lessons? There was no magic to it. Before anything else, Hendricks told me, he had to ensure that his "cabinet" of district and school-level administrators acquired a deep understanding of Flowing Wells' common focus. All leaders *had to go through the same training as the teachers,* and everyone had to buy into the new, more focused approach. As Hendricks put it, "Certain things were not negotiable." To work in Flowing Wells, every principal had to know and agree to uphold the common, research-based expectations clearly communicated by the central office. At all levels, leaders took pains to use the same common vocabulary to ensure a deep, unambiguous understanding of effective lessons and the research base supporting them.

At the school level, it all began with hiring—with the interview process itself.

Establishing Non-negotiable Expectations Before Hiring

When will we learn that one of the best opportunities for ensuring clarity and employee commitment to effective practices is *before*—not *after*—teachers have signed a contract? Consider how much time and energy we waste and how much unnecessary friction results from our failure to establish clear agreement on the organization's core expectations during the hiring and induction process. At Flowing Wells, prospective teachers were made aware early on that the district embraced a highly effective instructional model based on sound research. Here's how Hendricks described the process to me:

> We made [our research-based teaching model] part of the covenant with new teachers: if they signed a contract, they were committed to this kind of teaching. We made it clear that "this is who we are—what we expect. If you're not comfortable with this, you might not want to sign that contract." In this way, we established a culture where everyone understood exactly what they were required to do, but still had lots of freedom in how they taught.

Prospective employees were informed that every effort would be made to ensure their success, starting with training and followed by monitoring, coaching, and support.

Training and Retraining in the Focus Areas

Every year, the week before school began, Flowing Wells provided intensive training and retraining in the elements of effective instruction. You couldn't leave the district's training sessions without understanding and being able to implement the rudiments of effective lessons. All members of the faculty were required to practice, simulate, and demonstrate effective lesson delivery in a workshop setting.

Because (to quote Hendricks) "staff development breaks down immediately after you leave the warm glow of the workshop," initial training was reinforced in several ways. Under the direction of the district's professional development coordinator, all schools received ongoing clarification, training, and modeling of the elements of effective lessons at faculty and department meetings. Repetition and clarification were part of the fabric of professional life in Flowing Wells.

Moreover, each school included several lead teachers whose responsibility it was to conduct ongoing practice sessions and to assist any teacher struggling with the area of focus. Any teacher needing assistance was welcome to work extensively with these resident teachers (or, if they chose, with a teacher leader from another school in the district). In this way, teachers had extensive opportunities to rehearse—and thus master—effective practices before being officially evaluated.

Systematic, Focused Monitoring and Follow-Up

The monitoring scheme at Flowing Wells was a model of simplicity, repetition, and clarity. In combination, these elements helped to make the monitoring process less taxing for school leaders: because expectations were so clear and reiterated so often, teachers typically absorbed them almost by osmosis. Simplicity and clarity thus reduced friction and misunderstanding between leaders and teachers. As Marcus Buckingham (2005) points out, clarity is an *antidote to workplace anxiety* both for managers and employees.

At Flowing Wells, district and school-based leaders conducted classroom observations according to a regular schedule. Hendricks told me that these visits were typically *brief* and *targeted,* with the aim of assessing only the most essential observable elements (i.e., those in which every teacher had been amply trained and retrained).

Prior to any walkthroughs, administrators or designated teacher leaders should *reclarify, model,* and *practice* those elements of instruction that merit the most attention. If the walkthroughs continue to reveal the need for further clarification or retraining, leaders can bring up the matter at the next faculty, department, or team meeting (or at all three). If some groups or individuals need more practice than others, leaders ought to make it as convenient as possible for them to receive additional coaching from designated educators, including teacher leaders (who ideally receive release time for the purpose).

Flowing Wells' simple, redundant system of induction, monitoring, and ongoing support meant that a very high proportion of the district's teachers became highly effective. This was no accident. Consistently effective instruction was *a non-negotiable requirement.* Those unable or unwilling to embrace the district's model of effective instruction were not rehired the following year—but not before having received *every opportunity* to learn, relearn, observe, and practice the model. As a result, Flowing Wells maintained a high teacher satisfaction rate and very little teacher turnover.

Withal, the basic features of the Flowing Wells system were starkly different from the unfocused, token notions of much of what passes for current instructional leadership.

True Leadership vs. Pseudo-Supervision

Our failure to embrace simple, direct actions accounts for the prevalence of a kind of "pseudo-supervision" in our schools: a historic avoidance of frequent, meaningful monitoring and prompt, targeted feedback and support. We continue, against all evidence, to embrace the tradition of conducting formal, infrequent, preannounced classroom observations—and write-ups. To complete these, evaluators are saddled with dozens of ambiguously worded criteria, all of which are to be precisely assessed at the correctly calibrated level of implementation. For each criterion, the distinctions between levels of performance are often risibly arbitrary—written to create only the pretense of precision. Paul Vallas, the former superintendent of Chicago and New Orleans schools, recently criticized popular evaluation templates as "nightmares" borne of our "testing-industrial complex"; as he put it, the rubrics are so complicated that "they'll just make you suicidal" (Dreilinger, 2013, p. 1). The most commonly used teacher evaluation templates divert huge amounts of training time and administrative energy while failing utterly to improve instruction (Anderson, 2013).

Simplicity matters. Immense benefits accrue to those who severely reduce and clearly define the most effective practices and combine continuous, repeated training with *fair and focused* monitoring and immediate feedback or retraining. This simple approach increases teacher competence and confidence and reduces much of the guesswork, anxiety, and friction (if not hostility) that can plague the relationships between leaders and teachers.

Could Flowing Wells have done some things differently? Certainly, as all districts could. But I'm profoundly impressed by what they accomplished through an uncompromising focus on good instruction, by the pride teachers took in working there, and by a leadership that cared enough about its students to ensure, in Hendricks's words, that "all teachers were hitting on all cylinders on every lesson, every day."

Example 5: Orange Grove Middle School: Simple, Realistic Routines

I taught—and learned to teach effectively—at Orange Grove Middle School in Tucson, Arizona. My experience there allowed me to see—up close and with great clarity—how ordinary educators could also be highly effective instructional leaders. Orange Grove also gave me an invaluable school-level view of simple school and district-level leadership. As we've seen, effective leadership does not have to be overly complicated. It is largely a matter of

• **Determining and prioritizing** a severely limited number of carefully selected, highly effective practices.

• **Clarifying** those best practices and expectations—precisely and exhaustively.

• **Training and retraining** staff in the essential practices.

• **Monitoring** to ensure that teachers are meeting clear and reasonable expectations—and *responding immediately with targeted support* when teachers don't meet them.

Less is more. Exponentially more school leaders will succeed when we learn to exchange complexity and profusion with "simplicity and diligence" (Collins, 2001, p. 104)—when we focus on only a few things, and do so with "depth and intensity" (Payne, 2011, p. 47). The leaders at Orange Grove didn't have to be particularly gifted or inspiring; their simple system ensured that almost every teacher learned and consistently implemented soundly structured lessons. They also ensured something just as rare, and important: *that every student engaged in authentic literacy activities.*

Orange Grove proved to me on a deep, experiential level that ordinary leaders could achieve extraordinary results in very reasonable amounts of time—and, once again, without any additional funding. As a faculty member, I saw that none of the school's essential leadership mechanisms were burdensome or hard to master; I am convinced that the vast majority of school leaders could execute them successfully.

Like Flowing Wells, Orange Grove was successful because leaders focused on best practices according to their review of the research. Simple, easy-to-master mechanisms ensured that these practices were consistently and repeatedly emphasized, clarified, and implemented throughout the district.

A Focused, Common-Sense Hiring Interview

What a pleasant surprise: In my initial job interview with Orange Grove leadership, no one asked me to describe my "philosophy of education" or other such extraneous questions. Instead—within minutes—I was asked how much reading I planned to assign to my students, how I went about teaching a lesson on a book or poem, how many papers I thought were reasonable for middle school students to complete in a year (and how long I thought those papers should be), and what steps I would include in a typical writing lesson.

The interview included plenty of unscripted follow-up questions. Clearly, the aim was to get an accurate sense of how I taught English—and how seriously I took it.

The initial interview earned me a second one with the English department chair. She asked me similar questions and reemphasized that I was expected to engage in frequent writing instruction and that I would receive training in the core elements of effective teaching. Clearly, the principal and department head wanted to know *how I taught, how I would actually teach,* and *what my true priorities were.* And just as they learned my priorities, I learned theirs.

Clear Training and Clear Expectations

Before the school year began, every teacher at Orange Grove received in-depth training in the core elements of instruction and on the research base supporting them. School leaders reiterated that we would be observed and evaluated on the basis of how faithfully we implemented best practices. Here we got what we needed most: an unambiguous charge to focus on select fundamental elements and apply them to our curriculum. And we knew that in addition to our formal evaluations, we would be observed briefly but frequently.

School leaders didn't expect us to dazzle or entertain with elaborate lessons, projects, or gimmicks. They simply wanted us to teach worthwhile academic concepts and skills while consistently implementing the elements that we had learned in our training—for every lesson, every day.

The Importance of Department-Level Leadership

Departments—and department meetings—played an important role in clarifying and reinforcing Orange Grove's focus on effective lessons and traditional, college-preparatory literacy. The department heads at Orange Grove were and had to be highly effective teachers because they had to model effective lessons. In this sense they were true instructional leaders as opposed to mere coordinators.

The English department head made sure that most of our twice-monthly department meetings were largely devoted to instructional improvement. We watched her model specific, adaptable model lessons and learned to accurately score papers using our shared writing rubric. (This last process was new to me.)

Again, none of this was perfect; we would have been even more productive had we worked in course-alike professional learning teams, on course-specific lessons based on shared curriculum and common texts. Nonetheless, department meetings provided frequent reinforcement and reminders of the English department's clear priority: to prepare our middle school students to acquire the academic reading and writing skills that would prepare them for college, careers, and citizenship. It was made quite clear that students needed to do lots of reading and write *multiple substantive nonfiction essays*—at least two formal, multi-page essays per grading period—and that we would regularly teach each stage of the writing process explicitly and systematically, using a common writing rubric while employing the elements of effective instruction in which we had been trained.

Importantly, the ethos and agendas of our department meetings made it quite clear that our school wouldn't tolerate the excessive use of worksheets, movies, or aimless group activities (all of which consume precious time in most schools and across the subject areas). In this environment, where priorities were constantly being clarified, such activities would be out of the question. And though our students' scores were among the highest in the state, we spent absolutely no time on test preparation, focusing instead on *effective lessons aimed explicitly at helping our students become effective readers and writers.* I've seen very few schools with as strong a literacy component as Orange Grove.

Once again: what we learned in training was reinforced, communicated, and monitored regularly. As a result, my skills as a teacher increased considerably: I learned to make the purpose of my lessons clear, to know when I needed to break lessons down into small, easily learned steps, and to continuously check for student understanding (and adjust my teaching accordingly, during the lesson). In all of my previous teaching and student teaching, I had never learned, much less been *required,* to do such things.

Let's now consider two more layers of leadership that helped reinforce the focus that was emphasized and clarified in hiring, training, and department meetings: simple, systematic monitoring and quarterly performance reviews.

Systematic Monitoring

About once a week, the principal of our small school would make brief, informal visits to classrooms. These only required a few hours of her time per week—sometimes even less. I was always struck by how calmly and confidently she was able to conduct these walkthroughs. Her manner was a function, once again, of the clarity and common understanding we all had of the school's expectations—a clarity achieved through repetition, starting at our initial interviews, then reinforced during training and reinforced again during faculty and department meetings.

As at Flowing Wells, teachers knew that the aim of the principal's walkthrough was to assess the execution of *only about six* essential components of good teaching. We knew that she wasn't looking, primarily, for how creative or elaborate our lessons were, and she sure wasn't looking for evidence of dozens of ill-defined, arbitrarily parsed levels of performance criteria from any of the currently popular (but wholly unproven) teacher evaluation rubrics.

No: She was looking for soundly structured lessons taught according to the simple, step-by-step, "gradual release of responsibility" model in which we had all been trained. And because there were few surprises, there was less anxiety —for both teachers and principal—during walkthroughs. The fundamental criteria on which the principal assessed us were as follows:

• The presence of *a clear, academically worthy learning objective* on the board communicating explicitly to students what they would learn and how the learning target would be assessed.

• Evidence that the lesson was being taught in *short, manageable chunks.*

• Immediate opportunities for students to *practice or apply the learning* for each chunk of the lesson.

• Checks for understanding—to ascertain *whether and how well* students are learning each successive chunk in the lesson (e.g., by circulating as students engage in guided practice, having students hold up whiteboards with their work, calling on students randomly for answers).

• If necessary, *reteaching* or having students assist each other in pairs until everyone is ready to complete the work or assessment independently.

These points constituted the essence of instruction at Orange Grove. And though they took some time and practice to master and refine, we teachers soon realized that *anyone could do these things correctly*, even if our relative teaching abilities were and always would be evolving, imperfect, and unequal. Teaching according to this simple, concrete model enables all educators to vastly increase both the amount that students can learn and the speed at which they learn it (Wiliam, 2007).

When leaders expect and anticipate a high incidence of sub-par performance or aren't perfectly clear on what is and isn't effective, we all know what happens: we procrastinate or find excuses for not conducting frequent and meaningful walkthroughs. If we want to monitor teacher instruction effectively, we need to make walkthrough routines and their criteria as clear, simple, fair, and positive as possible.

Even so, leaders will still encounter practices that miss the mark. What did our principal do when our teaching *wasn't* up to par? She might have noticed, for instance, that

• Objectives weren't written clearly enough—or that the assessment wasn't explicit enough (a common failing).

• We weren't explicitly modeling and truly "thinking aloud" for each small, successive step in a math problem or a writing assignment.

• We were teaching too much material at a time and needed to break instruction down into smaller, easier-to-learn chunks or progressions (also very common).

• Some of us had slipped into old patterns of calling on students who raise their hands—and then moving on after getting the right answers from some students—instead of cold-calling, circulating, or having students hold up whiteboards to "check for understanding" so that *everyone's* readiness could be assessed before moving on to the next step of instruction.

When leaders observe a pattern of such practices, they can't ignore them or rationalize them away. They have to respond—immediately.

Immediate and Systematic Follow-Up

There are two ways building leaders can respond when teachers need additional clarification, coaching, or support: *collectively*, by addressing a schoolwide pattern of need at the next faculty or department meeting—which leaders at Orange Grove did a certain amount of, to be sure, though they could have done more; and, when whole-school (or -department) correctives don't suffice, *individually*, by arranging for certain teachers to observe and learn from a strong teacher (as happened in my case; the time I spent with my mentor teacher was invaluable).

Again: I'm a fan of addressing specific, schoolwide patterns of improper practice, one at a time, during faculty and department meetings. By *collectively* addressing these patterns, we make the need for improvement less personal—in the spirit of the "safe harbor" that was so effective at Flowing Wells. We allow teachers to self-correct in an atmosphere of greater safety and anonymity.

Collectively addressing unsatisfactory teacher behaviors saves leaders considerable time and, once again, spares both parties the prospect of unpleasant encounters that neither enjoys. In my own work, I've seen how much more effective and time-saving collective clarification of a targeted practice prior to a walkthrough can be than dealing with multiple teachers individually. But when subsequent walkthroughs reveal that certain individuals or small groups of teachers still need additional assistance, leaders can't blanch: they must meet with and arrange for those teachers to learn, observe, or be coached by an effective teacher.

And again: if, over the course of a school year, leaders did all of the above and a teacher still didn't improve, he or she would not be asked to return the following year.

The combination of training, reinforcement, and honest monitoring of a small, essential set of criteria had a salutary effect on all of us at Orange Grove. Beyond a doubt, it made us vastly better instructors. Schools that currently and consistently implement effective lessons or whose teachers require *generous* amounts of reading and writing across the curriculum might very well experience what I earlier referred to as a "Fosbury effect": large, immediate gains that occur—as they did at Brockton High—when highly effective practices replace their patently inferior substitutes.

In my own case, I'm quite sure that in the few short weeks it took me to achieve approximate mastery of effective instruction, my lessons were reaching at least twice as many students as before and I was able to cover half again as much material in the same amount of time.

Looking back, I think we could have judiciously extended our efforts at Orange Grove to address finer points of instruction—once we had truly demonstrated our mastery of the basic moves of good lessons. When teachers at a school reach this point, they might want to learn some of the methods suggested in books like Marzano, Pickering, and Pollock's *Classroom Instruction That Works* (2001) or Doug Lemov's *Teach Like a Champion* (2010). But until teachers achieve mastery of the basics, these methods will have a limited effect on learning.

Quarterly Performance Reviews

There was one more critical layer of reinforcement to the intentionally redundant system of supervision and improvement at Orange Grove, and it had as much of an effect as anything in the system: quarterly performance reviews. Each quarter, we teachers had a brief, results-focused meeting with the principal, who would review our gradebooks and other student achievement data. (Gradebooks were especially helpful, as they were an invaluable record of our most important assignments and assessments and of *how many students* had succeeded on them.) These reviews formed the basis of a short, focused discussion on current performance and ways we could improve it by the end of the next quarter, when we would meet again.

I must tell you: the meetings had an outsize influence on what and how we taught. Coupled with the frequent walkthroughs, quarterly reviews powerfully reinforced the school's highest priorities: reading and writing activities that prepared students for college and the consistent delivery of effective lessons.

Even a focused, 10-minute quarterly meeting can exert an influence on the innumerable daily decisions we make that directly contribute to student success. As Buckingham and Goodall (2015) note, an improvement-oriented quarterly review is an entirely different animal from the more typical annual performance evaluation: whereas the latter focuses on ratings, the former focuses on *improvement*—and gives the leader a chance to review short-term accomplishments, clarify expectations, reinforce priorities, and reward individuals and teams for reaching short-term goals. It is unfortunate that only the rare teacher today receives this essential opportunity *to review and analyze*—alone or (preferably) in course-alike teams—*and to assess areas* of weak or strong performance.

Quarterly meetings make vivid the connection between daily instructional decisions and our short-term results and lend urgency to teachers' work. The leaders at Orange Grove provided such clarity of expectations, oversight, and reinforcement in their walkthroughs and reviews that we teachers simply couldn't—and didn't want to—rely on worksheets, movies, or aimless group activities. We weren't perfect, but I can tell you that no English teacher at our school would have had students make posters of the elements of fiction, shown the full movie version of every book or story read, or spent weeks on a "literature scrapbook" (as my daughters' high school teachers did). Instead, we had our students *read, discuss, and write about the books, novels, poems, and short stories that they read.*

To this day, Orange Grove is one among only a handful of schools that I know of that require every teacher to assign and share at least two multi-page, college-preparatory, non-fiction writing assignments with a building leader every grading period. As David Conley points out, establishing explicit expectations for writing has more of an effect on college and career readiness than any other effort (2007). English teachers' gradebooks must further confirm that lessons are aimed explicitly at mastery of each element of the school's common, six-part writing rubric and that they are taught in scaffolded steps throughout the year.

The Transformative Power of Focus

It should be apparent that none of the good results discussed in this chapter would have occurred if teachers had been required to satisfy a profuse, confusing set of evaluation criteria or if instruction had been left entirely to teacher discretion. Nor would these schools have distinguished themselves if leaders had succumbed to market forces urging them to promiscuously adopt new "programs" or unproven pedagogic fads. The leaders at Flowing Wells and Orange Grove had the courage to embrace their "hedgehog" concepts and ignore tempting but inferior substitutes for the fundamentals of good schooling. They embraced instructional practices that Wiliam tells us are "20 times as effective as the most popular current initiatives" (2007, p. 186). And by being so focused, they had adequate time to deeply clarify, reinforce, practice, and monitor implementation of their priorities.

Takeaways from Successful, Focused School Leadership

The examples in this chapter provide a template for transitioning to a more streamlined and narrowly targeted approach to instruction in schools. Here are some takeaways to bear in mind when pursuing focused leadership:

• **Less is more.** Each aspect of improvement demands considerable time, especially in the early stages of implementation. This demand requires us to simplify: to severely reduce the focus of our efforts so that we can take the time necessary to clarify, train, retrain, practice, repractice, and monitor. We must learn to say, "No, thank you," to anything that takes time away from our very limited focus. For schools today, this may be the hardest lesson of all.

• **Improvement must begin with proven initiatives.** Leaders must base their actions on careful study of the research showing what works best—what promises, at any given moment, to have the largest effect on student learning.

• **Just one of the three core elements can have a significant effect on learning.** Coherent curriculum, authentic literacy, and effectively structured lessons: any one of these elements will probably have a profound effect on achievement—and in combination, they may be more powerful than all other factors combined.

• **Simple, consistent monitoring is essential to effective leadership.** Such monitoring doesn't require a lot of time, but it *must* be followed by immediate, honest feedback and support (beginning with feedback to whole staff and departments, and then—when necessary—to smaller groups or individuals).

• **Leaders must hold teachers to professional standards of teaching.** It is the leadership's duty to protect students from the ravages of malpractice by doing all in their power to replace teachers who can't or won't meet expectations with ones who do. Teachers should be informed that meeting fair, well-defined expectations is a nonnegotiable condition of employment when they are hired.

• **Additional funding is typically not a significant factor in effective leadership or improvement.** The fundamentals of effective schooling can be learned and implemented using existing resources.

• **Instructional technology is not a driver of effective leadership or improvement.** It makes no sense to train teachers in instructional technology before they have mastered the foundational elements of curriculum, literacy, and effective instruction. First things must be implemented first; technology is a *second-order* intervention.

• **Complex, multi-page "strategic plans" are an impediment to effective leadership.** The best plans are simple and focused primarily on the implementation of one or more of the three core elements.

• **Successful schools embrace the research that supports effective whole-class instruction.** And they reject the notion that each class must divide students into multiple, "differentiated" groups by ability, personal interest, or learning style. There is no strong evidence that this approach is effective (Goodwin, 2011; Finn, 2014; Schmoker, 2010).

• **Success doesn't require leaders to adopt packaged commercial programs.** The collective effect of these types of programs on student achievement has been abysmal. They serve only to postpone the implementation and mastery of the most fundamental and effective practices.

• **Effective leaders protect their teachers from an unfocused array of professional development offerings.** As Peter Block (1999) notes, once we know what works, we must *stop offering additional training*—until we have mastered and implemented our most effective strategies.

• **Leadership requires a Herculean commitment to "piercing clarity" and to repetition, repetition, repetition of "hedgehog" priorities.** Once leaders decide on a *minimal* set of truly proven improvement strategies, they must become "clarifiers-in-chief," unceasingly devoted to frequently and repeatedly explaining, training, modeling, monitoring, and (perpetually) retraining until no one can possibly misunderstand the core practices—and everyone can implement them successfully.

• **The greatest enemy is *distraction*.** The most critical practices are forever under siege by the forces of unproven educational innovations. As Collins (2005) writes, we must "exercise the relentless discipline to say, 'No, thank you,' to opportunities that fail the hedgehog test" (p. 17).

Discussion Questions

As a leadership team, carefully review the takeaways for effective leadership in this chapter, then discuss the following questions:

• Which of these takeaways apply to your school or district?

• Of those that do apply, which would have the greatest benefit for your students?

• What concrete changes will you make to apply to your school what you've learned in this chapter?

4

An Implementation Guide
for Focused Leadership

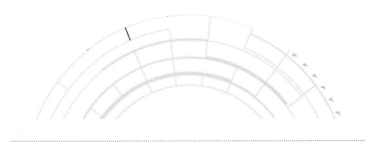

First, go back to the formula, preserve the core.

—Jim Collins

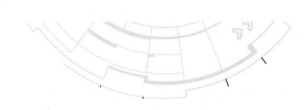

There is no single, lockstep script or sequence by which leaders can establish, implement, monitor, and refine the fundamentals of effective schooling. Context and evolving circumstances matter. That said, the following recommendations represent my best attempt to simplify—but also expand on—the combined lessons I learned from the schools and districts described in Chapter 3. Though I focus here primarily on school-level implementation, I hope that the implications for district leadership are obvious. Ideally, districts must commit to the fundamentals and then take concerted action to ensure that the processes in this chapter are applied at every school site.

Let's start with forming the leadership team.

Forming a Leadership Team

I recommend that leaders begin improvement efforts by assembling a fairly small leadership team of committed, like-minded administrators and faculty members at each school. The team can include department heads if leaders believe that they will support the initiative (which is not always the case). It is vital that administrators thoroughly educate members of the leadership team in the evidence supporting the importance of coherent curriculum, literacy, and instruction. Members of the leadership team are the allies and ambassadors of principals and district leaders, available to defend and explain improvement both in the beginning and beyond.

I encourage principals to pamper their schools' leadership teams, perhaps beginning by taking them on a short retreat and sharing the case for focusing on the three core elements. Thereafter, principals should meet with teams at least once a month to share vital, "ground-level" information that will help the team to guide the implementation effort and share successes. (For additional information on the rationale for assembling a school leadership team, see DuFour, DuFour, Eaker, & Many, 2006.)

Principals should ask certain members of the leadership team to help them with the next critical step: preparing and presenting the case they'll make for focused instruction, either to individual departments or to the whole faculty. In these presentations, it's not enough for principals simply to *say* that the three core elements of effective instruction are research-based; they need to cite and explain the research, and emphasize both the quantity and quality of their sources. Teachers then deserve a chance to ask questions and explore the evidence themselves. Principals might want to supplement their presentations with selected readings.

Once the administration has made the research-based case for focused instruction, implementation can either proceed immediately or be put to a vote by faculty or individual departments. If the latter course is taken and staff vote not to move forward, I recommend that any who *do* feel comfortable proceeding go ahead and begin implementation. Their successes should eventually allow school leadership to make adherence to the three core elements a new expectation for all faculty.

Implementation can begin by focusing on either curriculum —in which literacy is embedded—or instruction or by addressing both simultaneously; the leadership team can help with that decision. Once the decision has been made, I would suggest that teams make immediate plans to provide training for teachers in the components of effective lessons. In the meantime, I strongly encourage leadership teams to enlist a few course-alike teams of teachers to design a few simple, easy-to-mimic "prototype" curriculums that can serve as models for curriculums in all courses.

Creating a Sound Curriculum

The most effective curriculums are literacy-rich—that is, they visibly restore reading, discussion, and writing to their proper place at the center of learning. I would go so far as to say that any so-called curriculum that lacks such a focus on literacy is not, in fact, a curriculum. (For a more detailed treatment of how to build and teach a literacy-rich curriculum *regardless of your state's adoption, adaptation, or rejection of the Common Core state standards,* see Chapters 4–7 in *Focus* as well as the article "Simplifying the Common Core; Demystifying Curriculum" [Schmoker & Jago, 2013].)

Course-alike curriculums can be completed either at the school or district level—though in the latter case, schools should be allowed to review and provide input for the final draft. To begin the work, leaders should first ask select teams to build "prototype" curriculums such as the one in Figure 4.1. (See Appendix B for a reproducible blank template.) Effective prototypes promote clarity and help ensure that other teams avoid making needless mistakes.

The most effective curriculums are simple and straightforward, making it easier for leaders to monitor implementation. Any details (e.g., vocabulary to be taught, learning objectives) are best reserved for lesson plans or other supplementary documents.

If possible, curriculum work should begin in the summer, when teams can devote themselves to creating prototypes without distraction for sharing when school starts. Course-alike curriculums can be completed either at the school or district level (in the latter case, with input from the leadership of individual schools).

4.1 Sample Prototype Curriculum

History			
1st Quarter: "American Revolution"	**Topic**	**Text**	**Questions**
Week 1	Taxation without representation	Textbook Ch. 5 pp. 148–151	What were the best arguments against taxation without representation?
	Was the Revolution justified?	*Proclamation of 1763* (which forbade western settlement)	Was the Proclamation of 1763 fair or unfair to the colonists? Native Americans?

The Five Main Steps to Creating Subject-Area Curriculum

The following processes will ensure that all courses have a simple, literacy-rich curriculum. By "literacy-rich," I simply mean a curriculum that visibly restores reading, discussion, and writing to their proper place: at the center of instruction. Curriculums should be especially literacy-rich in English, social studies, and science classes, but also in mathematics, electives, and the arts.

As course-alike teams set to designing curriculum, administrators or their designees (e.g., department heads or members of the leadership team) must oversee the process, set deadlines, and support the work at every turn—obsessively, in my view. They should make it a priority to coordinate the completion of rough, serviceable curriculums for every course by, say, the end of the first quarter. (The course-alike teams at Adlai Stevenson High School had workable first drafts of curriculums in place after only four or five meetings that they then refined and formalized throughout the school year.) Administrators are encouraged to provide team members with release time—and, if possible, payment—for their work.

Step 1: Ensure that the curriculum is viable—that is to say, teachable within the time constraints of the 36-week school year (Marzano, 2003). That's about 180 days total—and, when teacher discretionary time and days spent on testing and assemblies are accounted for, about 35 days per grading period for teaching common curriculum.

Some simple calculations must be made when developing curriculum. Teams should begin by spending 15 to 30 minutes estimating how long it will take to teach each topic or mandated standard. To accomplish this, teams should do the following:

1. Use a pencil to mark every state or subject-area standard or topic with their best guess as to how long it would take to teach it—*with adequate time made for the inclusion of reading, discussion, and writing in the curriculum.*

2. Add up the total number of days it would take to teach all topics.

3. If a team's time audit reveals that it would take, say, 200 days to teach all the standards, then it must subtract about *60 days' worth of standards*—leaving only those that the team deems most essential.

There is no other way.

And take heart: by reducing the number of standards to a realistic, viable amount, the odds that everyone *will actually teach them* increase enormously. When curriculums are overcrowded, teachers tend to ignore them entirely and simply resort to their favorite topics and activities (Marzano, 2003).

Step 2: Allot the essential standards by grading period in a sensible sequence. Teams list the standards and topics in the first column of the curriculum document. Remember: all of this work is subject to revision as teams implement the curriculum and meet regularly to discuss its pace and substance and make adjustments accordingly.

Step 3: Match topics to texts. Once you have scheduled a preliminary, "viable" sequence of topics and listed them in a column, the next step is to match appropriate texts to those topics that are best taught in that way (as opposed to via lecture or classroom activities). Texts should be listed in the second column of the curriculum document, aligned to the topics and standards in the first. I recommend selecting texts that are *short enough to be read in class* (about one to three pages long), and that form the basis of the lesson itself. These can be taken from textbooks, periodicals, newspapers, speeches, and so on.

Once again: texts—including very short, targeted texts—should become the focus of a substantially higher proportion of lessons in all subjects. (In mathematics, texts can be in the form of word problems—such as the ones contained in the Common Core state standards for that subject.)

Texts should be selected thoughtfully, and can be selected over time rather than all at once; it's fine for teams to select texts only for the upcoming grading period and then to continue selecting them for subsequent topics at team meetings.

Step 4: Develop questions or prompts. The next step is to develop, where appropriate, *one primary question or prompt for each text* (to be supplemented with additional questions or prompts in individual lesson plans). These can establish the primary purpose of a lesson and form the basis for reading, discussion, and writing about texts. Some examples:

• What is your opinion of the main character in this short story?

• Evaluate the presidency of John F. Kennedy.

• What are the critical differences between karyotic and eukaryotic cells?

Questions and prompts are in the third column of the curriculum document. It's worth remembering that questions and prompts can double as ways to assess student progress without necessarily having to collect and grade every written assignment. Teams should develop questions and prompts in stages—*and only after teachers have actually read the relevant texts.* As with selection of texts, teams can develop their questions and prompts for the upcoming grading period before further refining them over the year. (In subjects such as science or certain hands-on electives, a fourth column is worth adding to the curriculum document for labs, experiments, or activities that correspond to selected topics or standards.)

Step 5: Establish writing expectations. This step is especially important—yet seldom found in current curriculum documents. Teams must determine how many *formal, core* writing assignments should be assigned by every teacher of a course, as well as how long each assignment should be (e.g., one three- to four-page paper per semester for 8th grade social studies). Establishing concrete expectations is the only way to guarantee that all students have the same opportunities to acquire the formal writing skills that research shows are key to college success (Conley, 2007). Teams might also set general expectations for the many shorter, less formal writing assignments that are to occur every week (e.g., about three short *writing assignments* per week).

Let's now specifically examine the English language arts (ELA) curriculum. It requires a different approach.

Designing ELA Curriculum

It's important that leaders avoid the trap of building curriculum around the exhaustive and discredited inanities of the established Common Core lists of ELA standards (Schmoker & Graff, 2011; Schmoker & Jago, 2013). Schools and districts are on firm ground when leaders concentrate on what even developers of the ELA standards are now telling us: namely, not to focus on the grade-by-grade standards for the present time (Coleman, Pimentel, & Zimba, 2012). Far more important instead to focus on simple, traditional literacy: ample reading, discussion, and writing around good questions and issues guided by "the three shifts":

1. Building knowledge through content-rich nonfiction;
2. Reading, writing, and speaking grounded in evidence from text, both literary and informational; and
3. Regular practice with complex text and attendant academic language.

Once students learn to decode, the best ELA curriculums have traditionally looked much like the one in Figure 4.2:

• **Column 1:** A generous number of texts—novels, plays, nonfiction articles, poems, speeches, and so on—listed sequentially

• **Column 2:** Higher-order questions grounded in the texts, to be used as the basis for purposeful reading, discussion, and writing

• **Column 3:** Days or weeks during which teachers are to provide explicit, step-by-step writing instruction and for which they specify clear, common requirements for writing assignments (e.g., approximate length, general focus)

From what I've seen, the test items on the Common Core ELA standards would be amply addressed by such a curriculum document.

One more thing: every English course should establish at least *one extended writing sample* as its primary mode of assessment for the year. A well-written expository or argumentative paper tells us more about a student's reading, thinking, and writing skills than any standardized assessment—bar none. Insisting upon such papers would radically reorient English instruction toward the ability to read effectively, to organize and support arguments, and to write clearly.

Establishing a "Curriculum Czar"

Unless curriculum is clear and easy to use and understand, few will actually implement it. To ensure clarity, then, I encourage leaders to assign primary responsibility for curriculum development to a single individual in each school or district—a kind of "Curriculum Czar" whose duties might include the following:

• Recruiting a few "tiger teams" to develop—immediately—sound prototype curriculums (to be used as models as others build their curriculums)

4.2 Sample ELA Curriculum

Quarter 1

Text Type	Text	Question
Novel	*Sisters/Hermana* by Gary Paulsen (Lexile—1150)	How does the main character change throughout the story? Cite examples from the book.
Nonfiction Book	*Can I See Your I.D.?* By Chris Barton (Lexile—980)	Compare and contrast the stories and what the characters have in common.
Article(s)	Teen Dating: http://www.sheknows.com/parenting/articles/819080/The-teens-and-dating-debate-What-s-the-right-age	What is the right age for teens starting to date? Support your argument with information from the article.
Speech(es)	FDR—Attack on Pearl Harbor	What did FDR mean when he said "We have nothing to fear but fear itself"? Cite examples from speech. What made this an effective speech? Analyze each paragraph for how it affects the reader—and why.
Poem(s)	"I, Too, Sing America" by Langston Hughes "Oranges" by Gary Soto	Compare and contrast the authors' message in Hughes's "I, Too, Sing America" and Soto's "Oranges".
Two formal written assignments	3- to 4-page paper about either book read this quarter 3- to 4-page paper on any 2 works read this quarter	

- Setting at least general deadlines for curriculum completion

- Monitoring and supporting curriculum completion

- Leading an "Approval/Review Committee" for revising curriculum based on simple criteria

- Reporting and celebrating "small wins" in curricular development (e.g., when any single course curriculum is completed, or as the percentage of completed curriculums increases—by department or district)

No teachers should have to build their curriculum, by themselves, for every course they teach. We've seen what happens as a result: confusion, overburdened teachers, and curricular chaos. If we keep things simple, we will soon be able to furnish our teachers with the most potent, time-saving tool we could give them: *a coherent, usable curriculum* that will make them exponentially more effective and afford them maximal time to concentrate on *how* they teach—on effective lessons.

Training Teachers to Deliver Effective Lessons

To begin effective training, school or district leaders should identify one or more educators on staff who can correctly execute (or learn to execute) the basic elements of the "gradual-release" model. Trainers should be able both to communicate and to demonstrate these steps as clearly as possible. If they don't know their stuff, their errors and omissions can multiply and spread throughout a school or district. All teachers—and administrators—should receive training. I always encourage schools to schedule annual summer academies where new teachers are trained and veterans have a chance to sharpen their skills (or learn advanced skills, without corrupting or diverting us from the fundamentals of good teaching).

Training regimens must include a thorough review of the research that supports the core elements of effective instruction as well as plenty of opportunities for educators to *practice and repractice* each element until they demonstrate mastery. Teachers and administrators should engage in such practice with their peers and take turns role-playing as students. Accurate feedback is vital during these practice sessions, with the goal of ensuring at least basic mastery of the elements by the end of training. Of course, no one ever masters all the elements or dimensions of effective instruction; there is always infinite room for improvement. The good news is that with good training and ongoing modeling and support, anyone can achieve *basic mastery* in fairly short order.

Monitoring Implementation of Curriculum and Instruction

Like it or don't: what gets monitored—and measured—gets done. Simple, focused monitoring is indispensable, exerting a positive force on performance and allowing us to enjoy and celebrate the short-term, targeted, incremental improvements that are crucial to collective progress and morale (Collins, 2001). There are two key strategies for collecting data on implementation: *weekly single-focus classroom walkthroughs* and *quarterly performance reviews.*

Single-Focus Classroom Walkthroughs

Every effort should be made to make walkthroughs positive experiences without any sort of "gotcha" factor. Leaders conducting them should be looking to observe as many teachers as possible doing the right things so that everyone can celebrate at the next faculty meeting before moving on to the next challenge.

To this end, it is important for leaders to focus on *only one element at a time* during walkthroughs. They may also want to review the chosen element with teachers or even briefly retrain them in it prior to walkthroughs, perhaps during faculty, department, or team meetings—or all of the above. Remember: repetition is key to clarity and improved performance. After training, faculty should be informed that leaders will be sharing walkthrough data on the specific element being assessed and only peripherally monitoring for other patterns of strength or weakness, and that initial feedback and opportunities for additional training will be available to all.

When it comes to mastering these fundamentals, I would suggest waiting to provide *individual* feedback until teachers have had an opportunity to learn from leaders' comments on their observations at faculty or department meetings. This maximizes the opportunity for teachers to recognize and correct their own shortcomings in a safe, collective setting. Moreover, these multiple intermediary efforts to model and clarify good practice will make it easier for leaders to take corrective action with individuals when the occasion demands.

Quarterly Performance Reviews

As we have seen, performance reviews can powerfully promote continuous, measurable improvement among teachers. Like good training and effective walkthroughs, successful performance reviews mimic the elements of good instruction, composed as they are of focused effort, checks for understanding, and informed adjustments in the service of short-term improvement. Reviews promote a sensible accountability, reinforce the importance of teamwork, and guide the faithful implementation of curriculum. Administrators, department heads, or teacher leaders can meet briefly to conduct such reviews with course-alike teams; in smaller schools, they can meet with and conduct reviews with whole departments or teachers in the same subject area.

Ideally, reviews should take into account student scores on common, course-alike assessments given each quarter —or major unit assessments. These don't need to be fully comprehensive—as long as they gauge a general level of learning over the grading period, they're helpful. They should, however, be adequately aligned with year-end or state assessments.

That said, curriculum-based assessments shouldn't be near-replicas of state assessments, with their overreliance on multiple-choice items. As much as possible, we should favor items and questions that require problem solving and writing (see Chapter 4–7 in *Focus*). Gradebooks can also be a rich source of information and the basis for productive, targeted conversations between leaders and teachers.

The review format need not be complicated. There's nothing quite as effective as cutting to the chase with simple,
direct questions such as these:

• How many students did well on major assessments?

• How does student performance compare to the last grading period?

• In what areas were students strong or weak?

• How can we help students improve in their areas of
weakness?

During these brief meetings, leaders should take a few essential notes. Afterward, they can offer targeted support and, if
appropriate, set measurable assessment or implementation
goals for the next grading period.

Finally: the role of team-based professional learning communities is critical to instructional quality and improvement.
The work of teams should pervade all that is discussed in
these pages.

Establishing Team-Based Professional Learning Communities (PLCs)

Leaders must arrange regular times—at least twice a month—
for teachers to meet and perfect their teaching practices.
Though most schools today claim to embrace professional
learning communities (PLCs) and may even adopt their
trappings, they usually fail to establish what ought to be
every PLC's two highest initial priorities: creating a clear,
literacy-rich curriculum for every course and ensuring that
all faculty master the delivery of sound lessons.

Once the PLCs have done this, leaders must remind them that their primary goal is *to develop and refine lessons and strategies for teaching the common curriculum.* Here are a few examples of actions that PLCs can take to achieve this goal:

• Creating lessons for particularly challenging topics or skills (e.g. writing or any of its essential traits)

• Refining and improving existing curriculum

• Developing and refining common, curriculum-based assessments that emphasize writing and thoughtful engagement with content

• Analyzing assessment data to assess progress and identify areas that need improvement

• Collaboratively assessing samples of written work to ensure a reasonable level of reliability and to refine writing instruction

• Creating "anticipatory sets" for specific topics, skills, and concepts to stimulate interest in the content

• Sharing and searching for the most readable and arresting texts to accompany essential standards, topics, issues, and concepts

• Generating rich, thought-provoking questions for every common text

• "Chunking" lessons into manageable steps, as well as identifying particularly difficult chunks and developing and sharing ways to teach them effectively

• Building whole lessons as a team and practicing them in a "lesson study" format

• Ensuring practice and overlearning of the elements of effective lessons and of selected proven, research-based teaching strategies such as those identified by Lemov (2010) and Marzano, Pickering, and Pollock (2001)

For me, these activities constitute the essential work of the team: they work from and build on the firm foundation of coherent curriculum and well-structured lessons.

Once that foundation is laid, and fundamental skills are acquired, it is the team that will account for most of the additional improvements in the curriculum and its delivery. I strongly recommend that leaders provide specifications like the above and then monitor to ensure that they occur—by dropping by team meetings, having team leaders keep brief minutes, and discussing such items in quarterly meetings. In the absence of such tasks, too many team meetings devolve into discussions of questionable value.

With all of these good things in place, it only makes sense that you would want to hire any new personnel on the basis of their commitment to such a system.

Hiring New Personnel

Throughout the hiring process, I would urge all school and district leaders to clarify that they will only hire staff who are committed to meeting essential expectations. To this end, leaders might want to provide prospective hires with

- A one-page summary of the school's or district's priorities.

- Samples of the curriculum that they would be teaching—and continually revising—with colleagues.

• A template such as the one in Figure 2.1 to give candidates a sense of the kind of teaching they would be trained
in and expected to provide.

Interview questions should also focus on candidates' willingness and ability to commit to essential expectations.

10-Point Summary Plan

Even crudely conducted, the simple leadership routines I
describe in this chapter would address the most primary,
critical features of effective schooling. For that reason, they
almost can't fail to have a significant effect, in the majority of schools, on students' academic and intellectual pre-
paredness. In the spirit of simplicity and reiteration, here
is a quick-reference list of the 10 major steps to ensuring
focused leadership in schools and districts.

1. Form and sustain a leadership team at the school or district level unified around the essential concepts of sound
   curriculum, literacy instruction, and lesson delivery.

2. Enlist prototype teams to build coherent, literacy-
   rich, user-friendly curriculums and common quarterly assessments for every course. Teams should set
   deadlines and celebrate when they meet them.

3. Identify selected teachers or leaders—preferably
   in-house—to train and overtrain all teachers and
   school administrators in the basic strategies of sound
   lessons. Teachers and school administrators are
   expected to learn and practice the strategies until they
   achieve mastery.

4. Create a summer program where teachers and administrators can learn, practice, relearn, and refine their knowledge and skills in the three core elements.

5. Frequently review the case for literacy-rich curriculum and effective instruction, supplementing with further evidence each time.

6. Devote meaningful portions of faculty and department meetings to true learning and practicing sessions during which teachers routinely—even redundantly—receive explicit training and retraining, as needed, in a given area of focus and watch demonstrations of sound lesson delivery.

7. Conduct routine data-driven, targeted, and unannounced classroom walkthroughs. Share observations with faculty as immediately as possible. Then either celebrate progress or take appropriate corrective action with all faculty before moving on to individual support.

8. Conduct quarterly performance reviews with teams for the purpose of gauging progress and identifying opportunities for improvement. Divide this work among administrators, department heads, and teacher leaders.

9. Arrange for all teachers to work in PLCs that meet at least twice a month with the primary goals of ensuring clarity about the common curriculum and helping one another to develop interesting and effective lessons.

10. Revise hiring procedures to ensure that all new employees thoroughly understand the school's or district's priorities and are committed to them.

Consider eliminating or suspending all programs and initiatives—or as many of them as possible—until the above fundamentals are mastered by all. These 10 actions are rarely embraced in most schools or districts today. For that reason, they stand to have a decisive effect. If we can learn to embrace simplicity, clarity, and redundancy—if we can resist the institutional inertia of educational fads and programs, and instead embrace and implement what is manifestly most effective—we'll be able to radically transform teacher practice and student learning. In this difficult and important work, I wish you the very best.

Action Steps

Action Step 1: Assess for Focus. In light of what you learned in this chapter, what additional strategies or supports might you adopt that would help you to enhance or ensure the successful implementation of the following criteria for focusing on curriculum, literacy, and instruction? What might you stop doing that currently prevents you from focusing fully on these criteria?

• A simple, content-rich curriculum is in place for every course.

• All teachers can confidently read, understand, and implement the curriculum.

• The curriculum designates the core topics and skills to be taught on a weekly or biweekly basis, with some room left for teacher discretion.

• All teachers consistently implement the curriculum.

• The curriculum includes a generous number of agreed-upon texts for all content areas aligned to core topics and skills.

• Students routinely read, discuss, and write about the texts during the school day.

- All teachers fully understand, routinely practice, and consistently implement the major components of effective lessons (see Figure 2.1).

Action Step 2: Plan Focused Action. Make a master list of potential actions you might take and arrange them in order of priority. Select only a manageable number of actions on which to move forward.

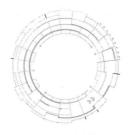

Appendix A:
The Elements of
Effective Lessons

If, as Marcus Buckingham avers, clarity is the leader's primary job, then all school leaders will get better results if they have a deep grasp of the core elements of effective lessons. The list here represents my preferred rendering of those elements.

1. Clear Purpose or Learning Objective. Research continues to stress the importance of clarifying—for any lesson—what will be learned and how the learning will be demonstrated (Marzano, 2007; Wiggins, 2013). The purpose of each lesson should be posted prominently and referred to often enough to help students—and the teacher!—stay focused and enjoy their sense of progress. For many lessons, a clear text-based question will serve as a strong learning objective. Students will need a clear explanation of the objective before the lesson begins. Teams or departments should be in charge of developing and refining objectives, and should record particularly effective ones for future use.

2. Anticipatory Set. This brief step helps students become receptive to the day's learning by explaining to them why it is worth their time and effort. Anticipatory sets can consist of background information, anecdotes, interesting or compelling facts, or explanations of how the lesson will prepare students for their futures. They also encourage teachers to reflect on the value or legitimacy of what they're teaching—and to consider whether it should be taught to begin with. Anticipatory sets should last about three minutes. As with learning objectives, teachers are wise to develop them in teams and record them for future use.

3. Teaching and Modeling. Once the above steps are completed, we can begin to demonstrate how students will acquire that day's knowledge or intellectual skill, i.e., through note-taking, problem-solving, computing, composing, close reading/annotation. None of these are ever learned once and for all. It is worth repeating that we must teach and model in *very small, manageably sized chunks, one at a time*, so as not to overwhelm students. Such teaching ensures that the maximum number of students will be successful on each step of the lesson. And it greatly reduces the number of students who will need additional assistance or tutoring at the end of the lesson.

For this step and the next, it is especially important that each step or chunk of a lesson is *aligned to the assessment*—and is necessary to its successful completion. I see many lessons that consist of a series of cute but only superficially related activities that aren't truly necessary to the completion of that day's objective or assessment.

4. Guided Practice. For each "chunk" in the lesson, we must give students an opportunity to visibly mimic what was just modeled, i.e., to practice with or process the new knowledge in a way that allows the teacher to observe and thus "guide" their students' practice. During this step, students must engage in observable practices that allow us to see visible evidence of whether and how well they are progressing, through such activities as (once again) taking notes, making calculations, attempting to solve or analyze a math problem—or a small part of a problem—annotating and underlining, composing a sentence or paragraph.

One more thing: if you want your lessons to proceed at a stimulating pace, and if you'd like students to work with greater urgency and concentration (and who doesn't?), always give them a specific allotment of time for each "guided practice." It will often be as little as one to two minutes, with reminders of how much time they have left. This applies to work done individually as well as pair or group work.

5. Checks for Understanding. As students engage in guided practice, we must monitor and assess their efforts and progress on that particular chunk of instruction—to make sure they are indeed understanding or succeeding with what we just taught. We can do this by cold calling on a small representative sample of students (or pairs of students); circulating around the classroom to observe student work, i.e., calculations, writing, or note-taking; by having them hold up whiteboards that allow us to scan their work and answers; by having students indicate their understanding through a simple, unobtrusive signal ("thumbs up/down/in-between"). Without such methods, it is impossible to teach effectively, as good teaching depends upon our knowing, for each stage of the lesson, whether our students are ready to move on or need us to adjust our instruction—by providing additional modeling or explanation, i.e., "reteaching."

6. Adjustments to Instruction. When we "check for understanding" we will often find that some or many students aren't succeeding after our initial instruction. Despite the temptation, this is not the time to frantically attempt to tutor each struggling student; other students typically shut down the moment they see the teacher spending more than a quick moment at one student's desk. Tutoring between steps interrupts the engaging pace essential to good lessons.

Withal: it is manifestly more time-efficient and effective to provide brief, targeted reteaching to the entire class—or to allow students to help each other in pairs for brief amounts of time. These strategies ensure what every teacher wants: a considerably higher proportion of students succeeding on each chunk of instruction.

7. Independent Practice. Once students have demonstrated mastery of each requisite step in the lesson, we can allow them to work independently to complete their work (a set of problems, a written explanation or argument, etc.). This is an excellent time for the teacher to work with/tutor those students who still need extra assistance.

Perhaps the most important, least understood aspect of such lessons is the middle steps—guided practice, checks for understanding, and adjustments to instruction. As familiar as teachers are with these terms, many haven't seen trainers properly model the essential middle steps (teaching, guided practice, checking for understanding/formative assessment, and adjustment to instruction). That is, they've not been shown that these elements are cyclical and continuous: that if there are 5 major chunks in a lesson, we may have to repeat the cycle two or more times for some of those chunks—a total of 10 to 15 quick, purposeful cycles—until students are ready to complete the day's task or assessment independently. We rarely see this in execution, even though this cycle *is the essence of such lessons and the reason they are so effective.*

Of course . . . there are plenty of details one could add here. But these are the essential details I believe leaders most need to get started.

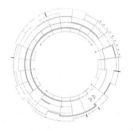

Appendix B:
Prototype
Curriculum Templates

To download printable PDFs of the prototype curriculum templates featured in this book, go to http://www.ascd.org/ASCD/pdf/books/ SchmokerAppendixB.pdf

Curriculum Map for Subjects Other Than English

Course: _____ Grading Period: _____

Week	Topics/ Concepts	Text	Focus Question/ Prompt	Activities/Labs
1				
2				
3				
4				
5				

Continued

Curriculum Map for Subjects Other Than English *(continued)*

Course: _____ Grading Period: _____

Week	Topics/ Concepts	Text	Focus Question/ Prompt	Activities/Labs
6				
7				
8				
9				

Number/ description of major papers _____

Approximate length of major papers _____

Approximate number of short, informal papers per week _____

Curriculum Map for English Language Arts

Course: _____   Grading Period: _____

Week	Topics/ Concepts	Text	Focus Question/ Prompt
1			
2			
3			
4			
5			

Continued

Curriculum Map for English Language Arts *(continued)*

Course: _____   Grading Period: _____

Week	Topics/ Concepts	Text	Focus Question/ Prompt
6			
7			
8			
9			

Number/
description
of major
papers ____

Approximate
length of
major papers____

Approximate
number of short,
informal papers
per week ____

References

Allington, R. L. (2001). *What really matters for struggling readers*. New York: Addison Wesley Longman.

Alter, C. (2014, September 22). 10 Questions/Sheryl Sandberg. *Time, 84.*

Anderson, J. (2013, March 31). Curious grade for teachers: Nearly all pass. *New York Times*, A1, 4.

Anonymous (2008, Spring). There's a hole in state standards. *American Educator, 22*(3), 6–7.

Beers, B. (n.d.). Personal communication.

Berliner, D. (1984). The half-full glass: A review of research on teaching. In P. Hosford (Ed.), *Using what we know about teaching* (pp. 51–77). Alexandria, VA: ASCD.

Berliner, D., & Biddle, B. (1995). *The manufactured crisis: Myths, fraud, and the attack on America's public schools*. Cambridge, MA: Perseus Books.

Bisheff, S., & Walton, B. (2004). *John Wooden: An American treasure*. Nashville, TN: Cumberland House.

Brosnan, M. (2015, Spring). Humility, will and level 5 leadership: An interview with Jim Collins. *Independent School Magazine*. Available: http://www.nais.org/Magazines-Newsletters/ISMagazine/Pages/Humility-Will-and-Level-5-Leadership.aspx

Block, P. (1999). *Flawless consulting*. New York: Pfeiffer.

Buckingham, M. (2005). *The one thing you need to know about great managing, great leading, and sustained individual success*. New York: Free Press.

Buckingham, M., & Goodall, A. (2015, April). Reinventing performance management. *Harvard Business Review, 93*(4), 40–50.

Burnton, S. (2012, May 8). 50 stunning Olympic moments no. 28: Dick Fosbury introduces "the flop." *The Guardian*. Available: http://www.theguardian.com/sport/blog/2012/may/08/50-stunning-olympic-moments-dick-fosbury

Calkins, L., Montgomery, K., & Santman, D. (with Falk, B.) (1998). *A teachers' guide to standardized reading tests: Knowledge is power.* Portsmouth, NH: Heinemann.

Coleman, D., Pimentel, S., & Zimba, J. (2012, August). Three core shifts to deliver on the promise of the Common Core state standards in literacy and math. *State Education Standard, 12*(2), 9–12.

Collins, J. (2001). *Good to great.* New York: Harper Business.

Collins, J. (2005). *Good to great and the social sectors.* Boulder, CO: Author.

Conley, D. (2007, April). The challenge of college readiness. *Educational Leadership, 64*(7), 23–29.

Copenhaver, L. (1996, May 13). Flowing Wells educator to retire but remains an advocate for kids. *Tucson Citizen.* Available: http://tucsoncitizen.com/morgue2/1996/05/13/195218-flowing-wells-educator-to-retire-but-remains-an-advocate-for-kids/

Corcoran, T., Fuhrman, S. H., & Belcher, C. L. (2001, September). The district role in instructional improvement. *Phi Delta Kappan, 83*(1), 78–84.

Covey, S. (1989). *The 7 habits of highly effective people: Powerful lessons in personal change.* New York: Simon & Schuster.

Csikszentmihalyi, M. (1990). *Flow: The psychology of optimal experience.* New York: Harper & Row.

Cuban, L. (2011, October 7). Denying the facts: Investing in computers and higher test scores. Available: https://larrycuban.wordpress.com/2011/10/07/denying-the-facts-investing-in-computers-and-higher-test-scores/

Darling-Hammond, L. (2010). *The flat world and education: How America's commitment to equity will determine our future.* New York: Teachers College Press.

Davis, V. (2015, January 15). 5 Fantastic fast formative assessment tools. *Edutopia.* Available: http://bit.ly/lxUUmOJ

Dillon, S. (2010, September 27). 4,100 students prove "small is better" rule wrong. *New York Times.*

Dougherty, E. (2012). *Assignments matter.* Alexandria, VA: ASCD.

Dreilinger, D. (2013, May 25). Former recovery school district superintendent Paul Vallas criticizes teacher evaluations. *New Orleans Times-Picayune.* Available: http://www.nola.com/education/index.ssf/2013/05/former_recovery_school_distric_1.html

DuFour, R. (2014, May). Harnessing the power of PLCs. *Educational Leadership, 71*(8), 30–35.

DuFour, R., & Marzano, R. (2011). *Leaders and learning: How district, school and classroom leaders improve student achievement.* Bloomington, IN: Solution Tree.

DuFour, R., DuFour R., Eaker, R., & Many, T. (2006). *Learning by doing: A handbook for professional learning communities at work.* Bloomington IN: Solution Tree.

Edmundson, M. (2004). *Why read.* New York: Bloomsbury.

Elmore, R. F. (2000, Winter). *Building a new structure for school leadership.* Washington, DC: Albert Shanker Institute.

Ferrandino, V. L., & Tirozzi, G. (2004, May 5). Wanted: A comprehensive literacy agenda preK–12. [Adventorial] *Education Week, 23*(24), 29. Retrieved February 22, 2015, from: http://www.nassp.org/Portals/0/Content/46537.pdf

Finn, C. (2014, May 7). Is differentiated instruction a hollow promise? *Education Next.* Available: http://educationnext.org/differentiated-instruction-hollow-promise/

Fisher, D., & Frey, N. (2007). *Checking for understanding: Formative assessment techniques for your classroom.* Alexandria, VA: ASCD.

Friedman, T. L. (2005). *The world is flat: A brief history of the twenty-first century.* New York: Farrar, Straus and Giroux.

Fullan, M. (2005, March 2). Tri-level development. *Education Week, 24*(25), 32–35.

Fullan, M. (2011, May). *Choosing the wrong drivers for whole system reform.* Available: http://www.michaelfullan.ca/media/13501740430.html

Fitzhugh, W. (2006, October 4). Bibliophobia. *Education Week.* Available: http://www.edweek.org/ew/articles/2006/10/04/06fitzhugh.h26.html

Gardner, H. (2009, February). Five minds for the future. *The School Administrator, 66*(2), 16–21.

Glickman, C. (2002). *Leadership for learning: How to help teachers succeed.* Alexandria, VA: ASCD.

Goodwin, B. (2011). *Simply better: Doing what matters most to change the odds for student success.* Alexandria, VA: ASCD/Aurora, CO: McREL.

Greenstone, M., Patashnik, J., Looney, A., Li, K., Harris, M., & Hamilton Project. (2012). *A Dozen Economic Facts About K-12 Education. Policy Memo.* Retrieved on April 6, 2015 http://www.hamiltonproject.org/papers/a_dozen_economic_facts_about_k-12_education

Hattie, J. (2009). *Visible learning.* London: Routledge.

Haycock, K. (2003, May 20). Testimony of Kati Haycock, president, The Education Trust, before the U.S. House of Representatives Committee on Education and the Workforce Subcommittee on 21st Century Competitiveness.

Henig, R. M. (2009, December 23). A hospital how-to guide that mother would love. *New York Times* online.

Hillocks, G. (1987, May). Synthesis of research on teaching writing. *Educational Leadership, 44*(8), 71–82.

Hirsch, E. D., Jr. (1996). *The schools we need and why we don't have them.* New York: Doubleday.

Hirsch, E. D. (2009). *The making of Americans.* New Haven: Yale University Press.

Hirsch, E. D. (2010, January 14). First do no harm, *Education Week, 29*(17), 30–31, 40.

Isaacson, W. (2012, April). The real leadership lessons of Steve Jobs. *Harvard Business Review.* Available: https://hbr.org/2012/04/the-real -leadership-lessons-of-steve-jobs

Jensen, B. (2000). *Simplicity: The new competitive advantage.* Cambridge: Perseus.

Jones, R. (1995, April). Writing wrongs. *Executive Educator, 17*(4), 18–24.

Kauffman, D., Johnson, S. M., Kardos, S. M., Liu, E., & Peske, H. G. (2002, Summer). Lost at sea. *American Educator.* Available: http://www.aft .org/periodical/american-educator/summer-2002/lost-sea

Lasch, C. (1995). *The revolt of the elites.* New York: Norton.

Leithwood, K., Louis, K. S., Anderson, S., & Wahlstrom, K. (2004). Review of research: How leadership influences student learning. Retrieved from Wallace Foundation website: www.wallacefoundation.org/ knowledge-center/school-leadership/key-research/documents/ how-eadership-influences-student-learning.pdf.

Lemov, D. (2010). *Teach like a champion.* San Francisco: Jossey-Bass.

Maeda, J. (2006). *Laws of simplicity: Design, technology, business, life.* Cambridge: MIT Press.

Marshall, K. (2003, October). A principal looks back: Standards matter. *Phi Delta Kappan, 85*(2), 105–113.

Marzano, R. J. (2003). *What works in schools: Translating research into action.* Alexandria, VA: ASCD.

Marzano, R. J. (2007). *The art and science of teaching.* Alexandria, VA: ASCD.

Marzano, R. J., Pickering, D. J., & Pollock, J. E. (2001). *Classroom instruction that works*. Alexandria, VA: ASCD.

Mathews, J. (2015, January 12). Why teachers should ask more questions. *Washington Post*. Available: http://www.washingtonpost.com /local/education/why-teachers-should-ask-more-questions /2015/01/12/84d60d16-962d-11e4-8005-1924ede3e54a_story.html

Mintzberg, H. (1994). *The rise and fall of strategic planning: Reconceiving roles for planning, plans, planners*. New York: Free Press.

Mitchell, R. (1981). *The graves of academe*. Boston: Little, Brown.

NASSP/NAESP (2013). *Leadership matters: What the research says about the importance of principal leadership*. Washington, DC: Author.

National Commission on Excellence in Education. (1983). *A nation at risk: The imperative for educational reform : a report to the Nation and the Secretary of Education, United States Department of Education*. Washington, D.C.: The Commission.

Odden, A. (2009, December 9). We know how to turn schools around— we just haven't done it. *Education Week, 29*(14) 22–23.

Odden, A., & Kelley, C. (2002). *Paying teachers for what they know and do*. Thousand Oaks, CA: Corwin Press.

Payne, C. M. (2011). *So much reform, so little change*. Cambridge: Harvard Education Press.

Pearson, P. D., & Gallagher, M. C. (1983). The instruction of reading comprehension. *Contemporary Educational Psychology, 8*, 317–344.

Pfeffer, P. & Sutton, R. (2000). *The knowing-doing gap*. Boston: Harvard Business School Press.

Pink, D. H. (2009). *Drive: The surprising truth about what motivates us*. New York, NY: Riverhead Books.

Pondiscio, R. (2014, June 26). Conscious incompetence: New ed-school grads are unprepared to teach—and we seem fine with that. *Education Next*. Available: http://edexcellence.net/articles/conscious -incompetence-new-ed-school-grads-are-unprepared-to-teach-and -we-seem-fine-with

Popham, W. J. (2008). *Transformative assessment*. Alexandria, VA: ASCD.

Ravitch, D. (2013, June 12). Robert D. Shepherd: Beware the social engineer and his abstractions. Available: http://dianeravitch .net/2013/06/12/robert-d-shepherd-beware-the-social-engineer-and -his-abstractions

Ripley, A. (2010, January/February). What makes a great teacher? *Atlantic Monthly* online.

Rose, M. (1989). *Lives on the boundary*. New York: Viking Penguin.

Schaeffer, R. H. (1988). *The breakthrough strategy*. New York: Harper Business.

Schmoker, M. (2004, February). Tipping point: From feckless reform to substantive instructional improvement. *Phi Delta Kappan, 85*(6), 424–432.

Schmoker, M. (2006). *Results now: How we can achieve unprecedented improvements in teaching and learning*. Alexandria, VA: ASCD.

Schmoker, M. (2010, September 27). When pedagogic fads trump priorities. *Education Week*. Available: http://www.edweek.org/ew/articles/2010/09/29/05schmoker.h30.html

Schmoker, M. (2011). *Focus: Elevating the essentials to radically improve student learning*. Alexandria, VA: ASCD.

Schmoker, M., & Graff, G. (2011, April 19). More argument, fewer standards. *Education Week*. Available: http://www.edweek.org/ew/articles/2011/04/20/28schmoker.h30.html

Schmoker, M., & Jago, C. (2013, April/June). Simplifying the Common Core; demystifying curriculum. *Kappa Delta Pi Record, 49*(2).

Schmoker, M., & Marzano, R. (1999, March). Realizing the promise of standards-based education. *Educational Leadership, 56*(6), 17–21.

Schultz, H., & Gordon, J. (2012). *Onward: How Starbucks fought for its life without losing its soul*. New York: Rodale.

Siegel, A., & Etzkorn, I. (2013). *Simple: Conquering the crisis of complexity*. New York: Twelve Hatchett.

Stotsky, S. (1999). *Losing our language: How multicultural classroom instruction is undermining our children's ability to read, write, and reason*. [New York]: Free Press.

Torbett, R. (2012, November 16). John Wooden: 4 laws of learning. *The Tribe*. Available: http://tribe.betterbasketball.com/coaching-philosophy/john-wooden-4-laws-of-learning/

Wiggins, G. (2013, December 5). Mandating the mere posting of learning objectives, and other pointless ideas. *Granted, and . . .* Available: https://grantwiggins.wordpress.com/2013/12/05/mandating-the-daily-posting-of-objectives-and-other-dumb-ideas/

Wiliam, D. (2007). Content *then* process: Teacher learning communities in the service of formative assessment. In D. Reeves (Ed.), *Ahead of the curve: The power of assessment to transform teaching and learning* (pp. 182–204). Bloomington, IN: Solution Tree.

Willingham, D. (2009a). *Why don't students like school?* San Francisco: Jossey-Bass.

Willingham, D. (2009b, September 28). Reading is not a skill—and why this is a problem for the draft national standards. *Washington Post.* Available: http://voices.washingtonpost.com/answer-sheet/daniel -willingham/willingham-reading-is-not-a-sk.html

Wolfe, T. (1987). *The bonfire of the vanities.* New York: Bantam Books.

Index

Note: Page numbers followed by *f* indicate figures.

About the Author

Mike Schmoker is a former administrator, English teacher, and football coach. He has written six books and dozens of articles for educational journals, newspapers, and *Time* magazine. His most recent book is the best-selling *Focus: Elevating the Essentials to Radically Improve Student Learning* (2011); his previous best-seller, *Results Now* (2006), was a finalist for the Association of Education Publishers' Book of the Year award.

Schmoker is the 2014 recipient of the National Association of Secondary School Principals' Distinguished Service award for his publications and presentations. He has consulted and keynoted throughout the United States, Canada, Australia, China, and Jordan. He currently lives in Tempe, Arizona, with his wife, Cheryl. Schmoker can be reached at schmoker@futureone.com.

Related ASCD Resources: School Leadership

Below are just a few of the ASCD resources available on this topic (ASCD stock numbers appear in parentheses). For up-to-date information about ASCD resources, go to www.ascd.org.

ASCD EDge® Group
Exchange ideas and connect with other educators interested in school leadership on the social networking site ASCD EDge at http://ascdedge.ascd.org/.

PD Online® Courses
Leadership for Contemporary Schools (#PD09OC07)
Leadership: Effective Critical Skills (#PD09OC08M)

Print Products
Align the Design: A Blueprint for School Improvement by Nancy Mooney and Ann Mausbach (#108005)

The Art of School Leadership by Thoma R. Hoerr (#105037)

Balanced Leadership for Powerful Learning: Tools for Achieving Success in Your School by Bryan Goodwin & Greg Cameron with Heather Hein (#112025)

Building Leadership Capacity in Schools by Linda Lambert (#198058)

Five Levers to Improve Learning: How to Prioritize for Powerful Results in Your School by Tony Frontier and James Rickabaugh (#114002)

Focus: Elevating the Essentials to Radically Improve Student Learning by Mike Schmoker (#110016)

Improving Student Learning One Principal at a Time by Jane E. Pollock and Sharon M. Ford (#109006)

The Learning Leader: How to Focus School Improvement for Better Results by Douglas B. Reeves (#105151)

The Principal Influence: A Framework for Developing Leadership Capacity in Principals by Pete Hall, Deborah Childs-Bowen, Ann Cunningham-Morris, Phyllis Pajardo, Alisa Simeral (#116026)

THE WHOLE CHILD The Whole Child Initiative helps schools and communities create learning environments that allow students to be healthy, safe, engaged, supported, and challenged. To learn more about other books and resources that relate to the whole child, visit www.wholechildeducation.org.

For more information: send e-mail to member@ascd.org; call 1-800-933-2723 or 703-578-9600, press 2; send a fax to 703-575-5400; or write to Information Services, ASCD, 1703 N. Beauregard St., Alexandria, VA 22311-1714 USA.

DON'T MISS A SINGLE ISSUE OF ASCD'S AWARD-WINNING MAGAZINE,

EDUCATIONAL LEADERSHIP

If you belong to a Professional Learning Community, you may be looking for a way to get your fellow educators' minds around a complex topic. Why not delve into a relevant theme issue of *Educational Leadership*, the journal written by educators for educators.

Subscribe now, or buy back issues of ASCD's flagship publication at **www.ascd.org/ELbackissues.**

Single issues cost $7 (for issues dated September 2006–May 2013) or $8.95 (for issues dated September 2013 and later). Buy 10 or more of the same issue, and you'll save 10 percent. Buy 50 or more of the same issue, and you'll save 15 percent. For discounts on purchases of 200 or more copies, contact **programteam@ascd.org**; 1-800-933-2723, ext. 5773.

To see more details about these and other popular issues of *Educational Leadership*, visit **www.ascd.org/ELarchive.**

LEARN. TEACH. LEAD.

1703 North Beauregard Street
Alexandria, VA 22311-1714 USA

www.ascd.org/el